The Sophisticated Hustler

When the Alpha Female Takes on Wall Street

Roselyn Keo

Printed in the United States of America

ISBN-13: 978-0-578-55532-4 (paperback)
ISBN-10: 0-578-55532-8 (paperback)

 This book is a truthful recollection of actual events in the author's life. Some conversations have been recreated and/or supplemented. The names and details of some individuals have been changed to respect their privacy.

www.RoselynKeo.com

Table of Contents

Acknowledgments

I have been through many ups and downs, but all the challenges I faced and all the blessings I have, made me who I am today. This book would not have been possible without the love and support of many people.

Thank you to my parents, brother and extended family, and especially my Grandparents, Mah and Gong, who loved me unconditionally when it felt like no one else did. The hustle and humility you taught me is priceless. Thank you for raising me and always watching over me, even from above. I hope you are proud of the woman I have become. I miss you guys so much. To my daughter Jazzy: you are the best thing that has ever happened to me. You saved my life and helped me become a better person. I am a stronger woman because of you. You inspired me to be the best Mom and I love you with all my heart. You're my mini-me and my little bestie.

To Chris, the love of my life: I couldn't have picked a better man to be the father of my child. We've been through so much and I feel so blessed to have an amazing man by my side. Thank you for being my rock.

To Kimmy, my ride or die chick: I always wanted a sister and you're the closest thing to it. Words can't describe the love I have for you. You are the best friend a girl can ever ask for. Your loyalty and kindness are is out of this world. I have so much fun when I'm with you. You're stuck with me!

To my long-time friends who I consider family: Anthony, Mercy, Anna, and Sabrina. I couldn't have done it without you. Thank you for never turning your backs on me. You believed in me and told me the "R" in Rosie was for Resilience aka the "Comeback Queen."

Thank you to my lawyer, Navarro W. Gary, Esq. for your advice and assistance throughout this process. I'm not sure I would have gone forward without your words of encouragement.

My writing coaches Adrienne E. Bell and Elam B. King: This was a complicated process; I didn't think I would do well, but you guys made me feel comfortable, helped me get everything off my chest and made the journey so much fun.

I want to say thank you to Jessica Pressler. Something told me to call you after you dropped off that box of cannolis. It was a crazy relationship we had throughout the years, but I'm glad it all worked out. Thank you for telling me I wasn't just meant to be a stay at home Mom. You encouraged me to tell my story and inspire others.

Last but not least, thank you to Lorene for your kind words, your personal stories, and your vision. You inspired me to get my truth out there and empower other women. I never realized how cathartic it all can be. Now I can truly say, "My life is like a movie"

Dedication

This book is dedicated to my Grandmother Kim Heak Aing, my daughter Jazzy and the love of my life Chris. Thank you for giving me the strength and courage to be a better person.

Foreword
by Lorene Scafaria

Screenwriter/Director ofThe "Hustlers" movie

No one is more excited to read this book than I am! Rosie's there-and-back- again story is as fascinating as it is inspiring. The book is full of insight, reflection, and personal growth. Rosie has written a tale of survival, excess, and the American Dream; with a keen perspective and raw intelligence. This book is for anyone who has fallen and gotten back up again. Whether you've read the article or seen the movie, if you want the bigger picture, look no further than
"The Sophisticated Hustler" by Roselyn Keo.

Foreword
by Jessica Pressler

Author of the New York Magazine article, ***The Hustlers at Scores***

"There's just something special about Rosie," one of Roselyn Keo's former Hustlers customers told me. "I can't explain it. It's like, inside that tough exterior you know there is this person who wants to do good."

The detectives had a slightly different take: "You have to be careful with a sentimental story," one said. "When I hear sentimental stories from people on the other side of the table, I have to take it with a grain of salt."

It was 2014, and at the time I was reporting The Hustlers at Scores, a story for New York magazine about Roselyn and three other women, who had been arrested and charged with drugging customers and running up their credit card bills at New York City gentlemen's clubs, or rather: "Jiggle joints," as the tabloids called them. That was where I came across the story. "Stripper Crime Ring Drugged Customers, Rang Up $190,000 in Charges on Credit Cards," was the headline in the Daily News. #MeToo was still a few years off, but the tone of the articles bothered me. The men were all made to sound like upstanding citizens, defined by their respectable-sounding professions: "hedge fund manager" "banker" "real estate lawyer" "cardiologist." And while all the papers showed pictures of the women—bikini shots, mostly, pulled off of Facebook—there was nothing from their side them that gave any indication of who they were, or their side of the story. They were just "strippers."

Which was not only, it turned out, inaccurate—it carried a whiff of judgment. If you have ever seen the 1995 movie *Showgirls* ("I'm a dancer.") or known a woman who worked at a club like Scores (one of the clubs named in the court papers) then you know there's no such thing as just a "stripper." These women are athletes, performers, psychologists, strategists. They are complex human beings navigating a world that is in many ways a heightened version of our own.

As a woman, on a personal level, I admire them: The personal maintenance has proven far beyond my own capabilities. And the amount of fortitude they must possess in order to withstand all of the gross advances, the long meandering stories, the corny jokes—honestly, there should be awards. It made sense to me, given all of that, why these women might have snapped. It was impressive, to me, how organized they'd been about it. And I wondered about the personalities involved, which were clearly being given short shrift.

Though it wasn't clear how much until I met Ms. Roselyn Keo. The first time I saw Rosie was in court in the fall of 2014. She was sitting up in the front with one of her co-defendants. One of them who must have told her who I was, because at one point, she swung around and looked me right in the eyes. Hers were bright and intelligent; alert—the kind of eyes nothing gets past—and it was clear I was being assessed. I don't remember what I was wearing, but I do remember feeling like it could have been better.

We didn't talk that day, but a month or so later, after I heard Rosie took a plea deal, I drove up to her house in Rockland County to see if she would talk to me for my article.

To be clear: I am not the sort of reporter who shows up at people's houses unannounced. "Didn't you worry it would be dangerous?" people asked me later. I did not. Maybe that was stupid but I think it was also Rosie. In that brief minute, we'd made eye contact I'd gotten the sense that she was not unfriendly. She seemed curious. Like the kind of person who was open to new experiences.

I'd brought cannolis, for some reason. Like I said, I hadn't shown up at any- one's house before. I mean, I didn't want to be rude. Everyone likes cannolis, right? "I don't like your nail polish," Rosie sniffed, looking down at my nails. But she let me in, and we sat in her kitchen and had the first of many conversations while her adorable daughter scrabbled around on the floor with Barbie dolls. Rosie's tenderness with her daughter was endearing, especially when paired with her tough exterior personality. At one point she talked about how she'd tried to mother some of the wayward girls at the club. "I offered to help them. "Every time you make money, I'll take it, pay rent and the car too. You can get a Honda for $200 a month. I'll put it in my name and pay it when you get paid. They never did meet me halfway and would be irresponsible," she said. "They wouldn't show up for work, they would get beat up and had to be in the hospital or had asthma. I was like, 'You have opportunities, you just don't take advantage of them.'"

She was smart, funny and thoughtful. She will tell you as it is and calls it like she sees it. Her analysis of the dynamics of a strip club was central to the article I eventually wrote:

"The reason why Wall Street guys party so hard is because they're not happy with their lives," she said. "You make all this money and you're not happy. So you go and ball out in the clubs to make yourself happy." Their lifestyle was quite similar to dancers. We make all this money and we're not happy with ourselves. You tend to spend and splurge to fill an empty void. It became a vicious cycle and sometimes you're not getting anywhere; you're just teetering."

And Rosie had a real way with words. "I want to start minimizing," she told me at one point when paring down her handbag collection. "Because the want of wanting is what's killing me. I need to decipher the difference between what I want and what I need."

So many great quotable lines rolled out of her mouth at one point I said, only half-joking, that she should write a Jack-Handy style book of inspirational wisdom. Of course, there's much more to Rosie's story than that, as you will read, in her own words, in this very fine book, which I can't wait for the world to read. Rosie and I had our ups and downs, but in the end, at the risk of aligning myself with the former customer I mentioned above—the sucker referred to in this book as "Gary"—I have to agree. Rosie is a special person. And there is a person in there who wants to do good.

"It's a fucked up story," she concluded, on the day of our first meeting. "But at least there's a happy ending," I said. "Yeah," she said, pointing to her daughter. "This is the happy ending.

People have questions, like, What made her do the things she did? Why didn't she make better choices? Why did she choose this road? What was she thinking?

I can understand it. Hell, even I'm intrigued.

CHAPTER 1

The Early Hustle

First and foremost, I want to be clear about who I am; **a New Yorker.** I'm very blunt and direct, either you love me or you hate me. Most of my family and friends think I should learn how to filter my emotional responses. But plain and simple, I don't have time for bullshit. What I say is what it is. If you don't like it, you can kick rocks.

I come from a line of work where a lot of people don't survive. I'm a homemaker *now,* but I used to be an exotic dancer and not just your run-of-the-mill pole dancer. I played the game the way it was *supposed* to be played. No matter the players, the circumstances, obstacles, or how stacked the deck, **I. Made. The. Money.** It was a lifestyle, and trust me when I say, it's *easy* to get sucked in. I met more people and went more places mentally and physically in my twenties and early thirties than most can say they have in a lifetime. But it was a mind game, and there was always an opponent. This was chess, not checkers.

Shit happened, and you always had to be thinking, strategizing your next move, and most importantly, staying ahead of the game. I became intertwined and all of it became the *norm*. Then it all came crashing down. Afterward, I buried that whole period and tried to just move on. To let the past be the past. But my previous life is now resurfacing. People have questions, like, *What made her do the things she did? Why didn't she make better choices? Why did she choose this road? What was she thinking?* I can understand it. Hell, even *I'm* intrigued. I'm a believer of the saying: "*Everything* happens for a reason", which is why I've decided to take this opportunity to tell my story in MY own words on MY terms, and I'll gladly take you on an exclusive tour.

I grew up—we all grew up—in a society where **men run shit.** Women haven't been able to be as vocal, proud, honest, or level with men, even though we have a lot to offer and work as hard, if not harder. We're used to continuously hiding and dimming our light to allow men to be the *only* ones shining. This was especially true for me. I'm a first-generation Asian-American, and I was raised by my grandparents in traditional fashion; keep your mouth shut and let the man take care of the family. That's what was drilled into my head from a young age, but even back then, I had my own mind. I wasn't so quick to submit.

Often, people ask me about what exactly my ethnic background is or where my family is from. I would like to think that means I'm exotic looking, which I consider a compliment. It's fun when people guess my ethnicity incorrectly because I could either tell the truth or pretend I was from somewhere else, like Hawaii. Being Hawaiian always sounded nice and exotic to me. I never wanted to admit I was from Cambodia because the Cambodian community is a small world, and you never know who you're going to run into.

My mother is 100% Chinese and my family speaks a Chinese dialect called Hokkien. As children, my maternal grandparents migrated to Cambodia from China. All of my grandma's children were born and raised in Cambodia. They had five girls and three boys. As they used to tell it, my grandparents were pretty well off, successful business owners. I heard of them having nannies, drivers, and housekeepers. It always sounded great to me! Hearing these stories as a kid, I would sit and daydream of how great my life would be if we never left Cambodia. But in reality, all of that luxury came to a crashing halt in the early 1980s.

If you know a little bit about history, then you've heard of the Vietnam War. To those who don't know about the Khmer Rouge, I'll explain it briefly. After the Vietnam War, a group of wise guys headed by a dictator named Pol Pot took over Cambodia and tried to make it into a communist country. They ended up killing approximately two million people, among them hundreds of thousands of Chinese immigrants, which the new regime stereotyped as capitalists.

My family fled and migrated to a refugee camp in Thailand. From there, they went to one in the Philippines, where my brother was born, then made their way to the United States of America. At first, my entire family was sponsored by a Christian family in Texas, but eventually moved to New York where they were told they could find an abundance of employment opportunities.

Baby Rosie, 18 Months Old

This instability carried into my early childhood. I was born and raised in Rockland County, just 20 miles north of Manhattan, but we bounced around a lot. My parents split when I was three, and while my dad visited my brother and I weekly at first, that turned into monthly, and eventually nothing at all. Meanwhile, my mom was working three jobs and I barely saw her. So my brother and I were mostly raised by my grandparents, who did the best they could, but they barely spoke English, and growing up with a cultural barrier was tough. I wasn't Asian enough for the Asians and I wasn't American enough for the Americans. School was in a predominantly Irish community called Pearl River. I remember being called "chink" and "gook" a lot. I had friends, but most of them lived in the next town over, which was too far to walk, and my grandparents didn't drive.

So I spent a lot of time around family. My extended family is HUGE. My mom is one of eight, and I have fifteen cousins on that side alone. My father is also one of eight, Cambodians who grew up on the rough side of Philly. Most of them are males. Being the only girl, I was teased a lot—the boys didn't want me playing with them. I remember always having to compete and always having to prove myself. They'd say, "If you want to play with us, you need to keep up." They would jump over fences, run fast, and try to ditch me. This wasn't so easy, I've always been athletic. And I was desperate to hang with them because I didn't want to be alone.

Even though I grew up in an upper-middle-class community, we always had less than everyone else. I remember having a small wardrobe of three pairs of jeans, one pair of sneakers, and maybe ten shirts. My brother and I had to walk everywhere. Growing up, I remember walking to and from school as young as eight years old. I always wanted my mom to drive me. Even though it was only about a mile, all the other kids were driven by their parents. All the other kids seemed to have loving parents that were still together. Seeing them made me yearn for what I didn't have. Having less than everyone made me sad. It made me feel like I was *less* than the other kids...different. I always had the feeling of being different and wanting to be like everyone else.

Our family *was* different. After school and on weekends, my grandmother would send my brother and I to the grocery store with a huge shopping list and made me pay with food stamps. Back then food stamps looked like Monopoly money. It came in a little booklet similar to a checkbook. She would make us buy a whole cart of toilet paper when it was on sale. My brother and I would argue about who would push the shopping cart because it was so embarrassing. And of course, we would always bump into kids from school. I was so humiliated.

Every year there is an Irish Day Parade on the street where we lived, Middletown Road. My grandmother would make me go in the streets to pick up bottles and cans. All that hard work and a full shopping cart equaled to about $20. Some kids had to clean their room for allowance. I had to hustle. When I was between nine and ten years old, I used to help my mom make donuts at a local donut shop. I learned how to make chocolate, vanilla, strawberry frosted donuts, jelly donuts, and powdered donuts. It was a family affair. My uncle was in charge of rolling out the dough and frying it while we did the rest. These orders were for the local high schools. We would box the donuts up and have them ready for pick up the next morning. I remember being mad and knowing how illegal this was.

Early on, I was the kid that laid in bed and cried myself to sleep. I would replay my negative experiences in my head over and over, then I'd get mad at myself for NOT saying or doing something back when the shit went down. By the time I was in middle school, the feelings of sadness turned into anger and resentment. I was the second child *and* the girl. In the Asian culture, that's a double whammy. The boy is the king of the family since they continue the family name, and the firstborn is always coddled and spoiled more than any other culture. I was jealous and envious of the way my mom treated my brother. Not to mention how she treated herself. I noticed that while she gave me the bare minimum, she always gave herself *way* more. She never sacrificed the standard she had for herself in order to make sure I wasn't lacking. I swore to myself I would never do that to my child. But first I had to take care of myself.

As I got older I became very sassy and fierce. When people wronged me in some form or doubted my abilities, I desperately wanted to prove them wrong. I began to have the *I'll show you!!!* attitude. I stopped taking shit from everybody and started defending myself. At school, this meant that I started getting into fights. I got suspended a lot. At one point I got expelled. I'll never forget what the Superintendent said at my expulsion meeting. He said, "We've never had any problems with Oriental students before, this is the first. I'm shocked."

Looking back, all of these bad experiences had their upside. The racist bullshit I dealt with at school and the bullying from my cousins made me tough—I had no choice but to grow thick skin. Now I have no problem stepping up to ANYBODY. And as much as I wanted my family to be like the ones I saw at school, growing up the way I did taught me independence. Walking to and from school taught me to explore and not be afraid to go anywhere alone. And my grandma had me hustling at eight years old! By the time I was in middle school, I was buying cases of Blow Pops at Costco and selling them to other kids for spending money. Having to do those things prepared me to have a good work ethic. It taught me that I was never too good to make money that was laying around and available for me to go get.

As time went on, my mom began falling behind with bills. We had no choice but to move and ended up in a neighborhood called Spring Valley. I went to Pomona Jr. High and Ramapo Senior High School, where the student population was much more diverse than it had been in Pearl River. I was thrilled. Everyone was cool and I had my main crew, my own little clique. My friends didn't make me feel inferior. I was accepted for who I was; race and household income didn't matter. The only bad thing was the curriculum. Everything they were teaching at Pomona Jr. High, I'd already learned. I was bored and wasn't being challenged, so when I was in class, my mind would drift away.

My mother wasn't as happy with our new circumstances as I was. Half of my new friends were black, and she gave me hell about it. I remember one time I was bumping the reggae music and my mom screamed at me for putting on "black music". Guess what, Mom? Those black girls taught me how to "drop it like it's hot!" I mean, what did she want from me?

As I watched my mother struggle, living in roach-infested apartments and settling for mediocre jobs, I came to view her as a broken woman, and not someone who was a strong role model for me. Even though she never gave me much attention, seeing her in that state made me want to work hard, buy her a house, have her live with me, and help me raise my future children. I wanted to show her the tough, go-getter spirit that lived within me.

My mother's side of the family is Chinese with a slew of successful college graduates and professionals. There are pharmacists, accountants, a doctor, etc. They are all about education and here I was a high school dropout, which made me the proverbial black sheep. They always said to me, "...doesn't matter where you are in life, your education can never be taken from you..." But school isn't for everyone, and not everything that can be learned is taught in schools. They don't have classes in street smarts! I had dreams and goals of my own. One day, I knew would do well and all of them would be proud of me. I felt sure was going to be something great.

Three days after my 14th birthday, I landed a job at Dunkin' Donuts making $5.15 per hour. Finally, I had money to pay for my nails, my own cell phone bill, and help my grandmother pay the gas and electric bill.

CHAPTER 2

Money Hungry

I wanted to be a teacher when I grew up, but when I realized how little teachers made, I said, "Oh, hell to the NO!" Too bad I didn't pick one of the most important jobs on earth. But I had dreams of making a lot of money. I know: They say money doesn't buy happiness. But I say: It's a downpayment! As I saw it, money could buy me everything I always wanted; a nice house in a great neighborhood, a fancy car, a fantastic wardrobe, and most importantly, freedom. I know that material things don't make you any less or better than anyone else. Your character and how you treat others defines the kind of person you really are. But in elementary and middle school, I noticed I was surrounded by kids who always had more than me. That created an insecurity within me, and I constantly needed to prove myself. I've been working since I was 14 years old. Aside from selling candy at school and working at my aunt's diner before I was eligible for a worker's permit, I was fascinated with the '90s hit show "MTV Cribs". Viewers had exclusive inside access to the lavish homes of the rich and famous.

When you watch a show like "MTV Cribs," you can either:

a. become a hater by saying, *Why them and not me?*
b. think to yourself, *If he/she can do it, I can do it too...* Or
c. ignore the rich, saying to yourself, *That house isn't that nice anyway*

I was always the "If he/she can do it, I can do it too" type of person. Seeing that type of lifestyle made me want more out of my own life. I'm a believer of the saying, *You can do anything you put your mind to.* It was so true for me. As a teenager, I noticed that anything I wanted, I had the motivation to get it on my own.

Three days after my 14th birthday, I landed a job at Dunkin' Donuts making $5.15 per hour. Finally, I had money to pay for my nails, my own cell phone bill, and help my grandmother pay the gas and electric bill. By law, I was restricted to a certain amount of hours but the manager allowed me to get away with more. He knew my situation at home and that I needed the money. And *I* knew that all I had to do was smile and be nice to someone to get what I wanted. Especially if it was a man. This was something I had learned at my completely illegal 40-hour-a-week job at Dunkin' Donuts: I had some power over men. Again, I was only 14, but men flirted with me all the time. There was an older gentleman in particular who worked at the BMW dealership down the street. He would come to the donut shop, speak to me often, and tip me very well. One day, he slipped me his business card and I met up with him at the mall during the holiday season. I met up with him to see if he could get me a job at BMW because I thought they probably paid a lot and I was money-hungry. I remember being so nervous. I was still a virgin and extremely naïve. I remember sitting and talking to him, then later jokingly asking him for $500. Guess What!? He gave it to me!!! I was like, "Wait, you're just going to give me $500 to go Christmas shopping and that's it?" I mean we *were* in a mall, plus, I didn't think he was going to do anything to me in public. Now that I look back, he was grooming me to trust him. I felt uncomfortable about the whole thing and decided to look for another job so I wouldn't have to see him again. But you better believe I took the money!

I left Dunkin' Donuts and got a job working at Footlocker which was huge for me. I no longer smelled like food, my pay doubled to $10 an hour, I had employee discounts for myself, friends, and family *and* I wasn't embarrassed bumping into people like I was when I worked at Dunkin' Donuts. At Footlocker, I befriended an older crew of friends who had cars and money to spend. We did a lot of fun things like going to the movies, bowling, shot pool at the local billiards, and frequently hung out at the diner after our nights out. There, we befriended Audrey, a short Trinidadian waitress with a sassy attitude. I remember her being funny as hell. She kept telling me I would do well as a waitress because I was outgoing and friendly, so I decided to try it. Whenever I landed a job, I was always on the hunt for the next best thing, always looking to increase my income.

Working at the New City Diner was my first real hustle. Audrey taught me to write the order for food on the second page, which was supposed to be the chef's copy, instead of on the first page, then to submit it to the chef, who made all the food. When it was time to write up the original check on the first page, I wrote whatever I wanted. This allowed me to hook my friends and favorite customers up in exchange for bigger tips. For example, if the bill was supposed to be $150 and I wrote a $50 check, the guest would give me a $50 tip. We both made out in the end and everyone was happy. At age 16, I was pulling in about $800 a week in cash.

It was the summer of 2000 and I was working a lot. When fall came around, I was back in school and juggling crazy shifts, working from 7 pm to 6 am and going to school from 8 am till 2 pm. I'd come home, sleep, do homework, and shower to go right back to work. It was crazy. Part of the reason was that I never wanted to be home. At the time, I was living in a tiny two-bedroom apartment with six people. The space was so small; if I could take a guess I'd say it was less than 1,000 square feet.

There was no living room. There were two decent sized bedrooms, a small bathroom, and a small kitchen; enough for a dinette set for two. My grandparents and uncle lived in one room, while my brother, mother, and I lived in another. I slept on the floor on an Asian-style bamboo mat. I was miserable and needed to get out ASAP. Eventually, I decided that the goals I needed to achieve—buying a car and getting an apartment—were more important than anything, so I dropped out of high school to continue working full time. All I wanted was to be happy and comfortable. As my grandparents aged, they had to leave us and move into an assisted living facility. This was when the wild side of me came out.

The type of crowd I served while working at the diner depended on the time of day. When I worked the dinner shift, I mostly served couples and families. Late at night, it was a party crowd of drunks, bartenders and dancers from *Lace*, the area's only topless bar. That was the shift where I met two guys who ended up changing the course of my life. I can't remember exactly what they looked like. Fat? Bald? Dorky? Probably all of the above. But I remember what they said: "What are you doing here? You're so hot. We just came from *Lace*. If you were there, I would have given you ALL my money." And I remember the tip they left: $50 on a $25 check.

Growing up I followed the show, "*G-String Divas*" and I saw how much money they were making. But I didn't think any of the girls from the show were pretty. I was decent looking; better looking than them, at least. *Maybe I could do something like that?* Of course, at 16 years old, I was way underage. "That's too bad," one of the diner guys said. But a seed had been planted.

I never danced completely naked. Some girls wore skimpy dresses and see-through stuff. That wasn't my style; I liked to wear dresses that left something to the imagination. From that point forward, the sophisticated hustler was born.

CHAPTER 3

Training Day

18-year-old Rosie.

By now, I'm about 16 turning 17 years old and the year is 2001.

I was no stranger to hard work. I knew what it meant to make an honest dollar. However, I was on my way to figuring out how to make a quick one. By now, I'm about 16 or 17 years old and it's 2001. I attended an audition at the same local strip club the man at the diner mentioned, called *Lace* in West Nyack, NY. My Filipina friend, Grace, was a lifesaver. She let me use her identification to work there. Like a scene out of the movie *The Players Club*, I was nervous as hell, scared, and intimidated. It takes a lot of balls to dance naked on stage for an audience. The veteran girls were very supportive and taught me everything I needed to know. I remember sitting at the bar, drinking tequila to cut through the anxiety, and taking notes from the girls on stage so I could mimic what they were doing. Drinking brought out that 'I don't give a fuck' attitude. What 16-year-old do you know starting a career as a stripper is super confident? When it was my turn, I said, "fuck it," and hopped off my seat to hit the stage. The stage was an elevated square wooden platform, like the kind they use to auction cattle, with a seedy strip of white lights stapled to the end of it. I requested to dance to a hip-hop song and the DJ played, 'Hot in Herre' by Nelly. I was drinking tequila to loosen me up. Then when I got the courage to get up there, I was dancing as if I was in my room naked in front of the mirror. I saw a few guys just gawking and staring at me. I noticed the car company logos on their shirts, they were service guys from the car dealership down the road. It was not fun at all. I was mortified and I hated it. I remember going home and crying. But I told myself to give it a full week. I quickly learned to adapt after a full work week. I worked about 4-5 days a week. As time went by, the more I was told I was beautiful it made me feel good. The money was good and my confidence along with income increased as time went on. The stage name I chose was 'Lena'. Lena is my Cambodian name and one I would easily answer to. I auditioned for Gus, the club manager. Gus wasn't the kind of guy to gawk at me. He seemed very by the book and all business. He was a bit grumpy and he looked like an older Seth Rogan. Gus was in his 50s and had shaggy brown hair with a medium build. He wasn't good looking and he wasn't ugly. But he was intimidating. I knew I wasn't going to just smile and charm my way through with him. I was so nervous when he was around.

I watched the veterans and studied them, that's how I learned the game. I already knew how to dance and I learned how to be sultry and sexy from watching *G-String Divas.* I tried to embody the persona of a dancer. My first performance, I wore a short dress with a pink swirl print I bought everything I needed from the House Mom; Dress, shoes, garter belt, and g-strings. It was like buying a work uniform. The House Mom was like the mother hen of the club, she provides dancers with supplies in exchange for tips. At some clubs, she was a former stripper who didn't want to leave the business completely. In other clubs, she was a regular chick. At *Lace*, she was a woman by the name of Leslie. Leslie was in her mid-40s and we looked to her as a mother figure. I remember her with blonde hair, 5'2, and chubby build. She also sold flat irons, curling irons, makeup, lotions, and accessories. There was a Brazilian woman who made dresses for dancers. She would come in with a full rack of outfits and sold them at the club. Everything I needed was there. Everything except natural ***courage.*** The other girls and the house mom became my friends and my job became my social life. Over time, I honed my routine and my persona. I never danced completely naked. Some girls wore skimpy dresses and see-through stuff. That wasn't my style; I liked to wear dresses that left something to the imagination. From that point forward, ***the sophisticated hustler*** was born.

While working at *Lace*, I met Angelo Rossi, who was the General Manager in training. We got along well since we both started working on the same day. I was 16 turning 17 and I had to learn the game fast. The customers were your locals. Middle age men during the week and young party crowd of 21-year-olds during the weekend. Down the street were a bunch of car dealerships and most of the men came in after work for a beer. I learned the art of talking and trying to squeeze as much as

I could out of them. These were your paycheck to paycheck guys. They weren't ballers. They spent what they could afford. It was challenging but I definitely make about $2,000 on an average week give or take. I learned good conversation here. Most of the men just wanted to talk and paid you what they could. The place was quiet during the week so you wanted to talk and drink to kill some time because you couldn't leave until 3 am and last call was at 3:30 am. I learned the art of good conversation at *Lace*. I learned to approach men and not to be shy. Anyway, since I previously dropped out of high school, I decided to get my GED at the age of 18. Then I later attended Berkeley College when I was 20. I walked out of *Lace* an underaged baby but walked out *a fully-grown woman*. I knew there was more money to be made in New York City. The house fees were intimidating in NYC; some of the club fees being close to $250 or higher. I was used to paying $30 to the club, $15 to the DJ, and $10 to the House Mom. But, it was time to take off my "training wheels". I felt ready to take on the Big Apple.

Once I discovered what the customer needed on an emotional level, I'd transform into just that. I toyed with their mental and emotional state to get what I wanted. It was like the girls always told me, If you don't, someone else will.

CHAPTER 4

Liquid Courage

After deciding to take on The Big Apple, I landed a job at a club called *Flashdancers*. The club was located on Broadway in the heart of Times Square, directly across from the studio where they filmed *The David Letterman Show*. I chose *Flashdancer's* because I knew a girl who worked there. It can be intimidating working in the city. I was extremely nervous when it was time for my audition, having so many people around was intimidating. But nothing great comes with ease or from staying inside your comfort zone. There were about 100 people in the room and *everyone* was staring at me. I remember seeing a lot of suits and more guys than what I was used to at 7 pm. Being on stage at a whole new club was like having to audition all over again. It's never easy being the new girl. It's that same feeling I had every time I had to start a new school; the butterflies in my tummy and the sweaty palms. Seeing everyone watch and stare, you wonder what they're thinking and if they will be nice or not. Even though I was nervous, I nailed the audition and got the job.

Sometimes there were as many as 90 girls working on any given night. The number of customers a night was larger than I was used to. It wasn't harder than *Lace*, there were just more people and I just had to adjust. I knew more people meant more money. It was just what I wanted, a better opportunity to make more money. Due to the location, *Flashdancers* had a different and interesting crowd: It was a mixture of tourists, locals, and professionals who stopped in for a drink. Every night, there was stage work and this required a three-song set. The DJ would run a music rotation of the music genre of your choice, and each dancer that was scheduled for stage work had to get up there and work the crowd. When it was my turn for stage work, hip-hop was always my choice. I chose artists from Mariah Carey to Jay-Z. But it was mainly a table dance type of club. We had to approach the customers, asking if they wanted a dance. We were left with no choice but to be aggressive and quick. My strategy was to talk to the men first then ask them if they wanted a dance. It was pretty effective and far less pressure than walking around begging men to pay me for a dance. *Flashdancers* was always packed so it was fairly easy to make a quick $1,000. Each song would play for 3 minutes, at $20 per song. My goal was to get $100 worth of dances out of 10 men. I'd always start my dances at the top of each song so I wouldn't have to spend more time dancing than I needed to. *Flashdancers* also differed from *Lace* in that the club had a lucrative Champagne Room, which is a private room that customers paid an hourly rate for, in addition to an hourly fixed rate for dancers of their choice. It was a small room with beaded curtains you could peer into when walking by. This was a good thing because it meant nobody could get up to any funny business.

Flashdancers was strict. The managers ran a tight ship; very *by the book.* They distributed W-2s while other clubs gave out 1099s because the dancers were considered employees of the club. There were also weekly schedules and working holidays was a requirement. If I missed a day of work, I had to pay a fine of $75-$100. If I missed a holiday there was a $500 fine. But it was also one of the cleanest clubs I've ever come across. There was absolutely **no** sexual activities or dirty grinding allowed. If anyone was engaging in that sort of behavior, the bouncers would stop them immediately! This was one of my favorite things about this establishment; I knew I wouldn't be placed in any uncomfortable situations. At the same time, it meant that you really had to hustle to keep customers interest. Every night was different, and I never knew what I'd make or who I'd meet. It was all a gamble. On a bad night, I would end up making $500. But it cost me $250 just to work. Every girl had to pay that $250, no exceptions! So it was really only $250. On a good night, I made anywhere from $1,000 to $3,000. All it took was one guy to make my night very profitable.

During my time at *Flashdancers,* I discovered my talent: The gift of gab. I was raised around a few men, which worked out to my advantage when I became a stripper. I knew how to mesmerize men with my ability to be sexy and speak their language simultaneously. I made it a priority to know teams, specific players, who was injured, how this would affect the next game, and who was out for the season. I also knew a thing or two about cars. I had a green Civic hatchback stick shift, with a GSR motor under the hood. This seemed to impress men who found me easy to connect with and engage in effortless conversation. That was my *superpower*.

To be honest, it went a little bit to my head. Not only did I not have to prostitute myself, I was a dancer that most of the time I didn't even have to dance. *Ninety-nine percent of the time, I got paid just to talk.* I used it to my advantage to get what I wanted. **Money**. I liked the attention. I mean, *everyone* likes attention. But looking back, I think I was especially seduced because of the lack of attention I had growing up. My parents didn't raise or praise me. And my extended family expressed their disapproval after I dropped out of school. So when I got the attention from the men at the club, it felt good.

Everyone at the club had a story of why they were there, whether it was true or not. My story was real, but I was careful not to give out too much detailed information: We'd all heard stories of girls who were stalked. My stage name was Elaina, another variation on Lena, my Cambodian name. Elaina was a student attending Berkeley College for Healthcare Management, which I was at the time as well. As it turned out, my family's emphasis on education had been pretty ingrained. Although supporting myself was still my main goal, I chose Healthcare Administration because I was good at management, and the stability of healthcare appealed to me. I'd thought of being a nurse but knew it wasn't really for me. It takes a truly special person to commit themselves to school. I chose working over school because I needed instant gratification. I knew I had to choose between working and school because I didn't have the time or discipline to commit to both. My mindset was to stack my money and go back to school later. School would always be there, but the money wouldn't. At *Flashdancers*, I made my monthly tuition in one week. I couldn't make the money without drinking. Ever since that first day at *Lace*, I'd been numbing my nervousness and fear of rejection with shots of tequila. Patrón had become my drink of choice. When I drank, I was fearless! I could approach anyone and have a conversation. In time, the heavy drinking and long nights would catch up with me. But early on, the money was like a drug that kept me going.

At work, Elaina became known as a *heavy hitter*. I was one of the top moneymakers in the club and had big scores every night. I loved the attention. It was all eyes on me and the men adored me. I had a sixth sense about guys who had money. I could tell just by the watch, shoes, or clothes they wore. I was a people person and I could read them while I was working them. I ended up with a long list of high-rolling clientele and regulars. I was intentional about scheduling my clients accordingly so I could make money every night of the week.

Every night I wrote down my earnings in my planner. I'm a visual person so I needed to see the numbers and whether or not there were specific days that I consistently made more money than others. No matter how much alcohol I consumed, I never got the numbers wrong. But there was no pattern or consistency; no rhyme or reason. You just had to be in it to win it.

I was very diligent and organized with the rotation of my Rolodex. I was a ***sophisticated hustler*** who had a lot of haters at work because I was doing the job right. The hate gave me the fuel to endure the fire. I was also a flashy kind of girl. I always had an appetite for nice cars and rims. There was nothing modest about me. I had regulars at *Flashdancers*, men who wanted to see me each time they came in. I always attracted the sad type. Some of them seemed to want me on more of a personal level *outside* the club. The ones who actually wanted me as their girlfriend were relentless in their pursuit to secure a relationship with me. I would feed them lines like, "I've been hurt before", "I don't trust guys", "If you really want me to date you, you would have to really work at it. It's gonna take time and patience." My customers, better known as "custys", were persistent, non-aggressive, and willing to be "patient" while paying me *very well* for my time. Some of them dated dancers in the past so they knew the rules but also believed I was attainable. I got to know some of them, the *real* them. Once I discovered what the customer needed on an emotional level, I'd transform into just that. I toyed with their mental and emotional state to get what I wanted. It was like the girls always told me, *If you don't, someone else will.*

Working in the strip clubs didn't help me in the relationship department. I saw the worst in men. I was seeing the scum of the earth. The ones who had wedding rings were the ones trying to get my number or the ones asking me out the most. These men were asking for trouble. I swear you'd think some of these men liked to get abused. I had one customer who would come in, buy me a drink, and literally give me whatever money he had on him. No table dances or talking, he just gave me his money with no questions asked. How much money he gave me would determine how much time I'd spend at the bar with him. He knew that in order to monopolize my time, he had to pay. **Period.** Otherwise, I would leave him at the bar because at the end of the day I was about my money.

My regulars usually didn't have a lot of money; maybe $100k to their names, 10k in the bank, or they had 401ks they'd empty out just for me. I say *only* 100k because there were high rollers who came into the club. I'm talking CEO types; men who would easily blow 5-10k a night on their girls. There was a time when I wasn't so fortunate. I hadn't yet lucked up on a big spender. I had to work for the money and it wasn't like they would outright give me 100k. I had to invest a piece of myself emotionally into these men. I had to make them feel safe by appealing to their needs.

Overall, it was a process. It took time. I dealt with the emotional side of these men. Most of them had mommy issues. Some of my custys were abused in some form or another by their mothers and had other assorted horror stories. Maybe that's why they were there, looking for love in the wrong place. Not that I am judging. A lot of us dancers had daddy issues and that's why some of us were there, possibly on the hunt for the same thing. Myself, I didn't trust men. I loved the attention I got from them, and I needed the validation to make me happy. Because my dad had left me, I was always the one to leave a relationship.

But my issues went deeper than that. As a child, I was molested by several male family members. When it first happened, I felt angry and hated myself. I felt like I lost control of the situation. I asked myself, ***"Why didn't you leave? Why did you let yourself get into this?"*** I felt powerless and controlled by men. When I became a dancer, I never once felt like I lost my power. In fact, it *gave* me power and made me feel powerful over men. In the beginning when things were good and the money was flowing, **having control over men made feel powerful.**

Experiences with sexual assault weren't unusual in that line of work. Not that we were all sitting around in the dressing room talking about our experiences with sexual assault. But I read somewhere that statistically, eight out of ten women working in strip clubs were sexually abused, and this was not at all surprising to me. Sometimes the commonality you have with another person is on another level. It's not a similarity of the same favorite color or movie. It's almost as if your desires or needs from deep down inside, connect.

At work, there were some girls who bragged about their customers buying them cars, houses, and apartments in Central Park West. I was like, *Damn, why couldn't I meet a guy like that?!* I always wondered how those girls were able to pull that off. For my part, I was happy to use my tragic past with my customers, playing the part of the "broken and battered girl" who doesn't date anymore because "I've been so hurt in the past". I became ruthless and quite sinister. I didn't care for the clingy and whiny clients, they were too draining. They would vent to me, talk about their family drama with me, etc. Especially the married ones, I was practically their psychologist. As draining as they were, that's also how I became irresistible to them.

I never aimed to be a homewrecker. My home was wrecked when I was three years old and I vowed to never do that to anyone no matter how painful my situation was. Why should I settle to be the other woman?

Women who are perfectly fine being the side chick don't love themselves. I'll be damned if I am someone's sloppy seconds! A nice way to get rid of them without making them feel bad was the old "It's not you, it's me" conversation. I was a pro at turning down guys nicely and still getting what I wanted. Most of my regulars bought the story I told and ran with it, thinking I was broken and needed to be saved. They would allow me to bleed them dry financially in an effort to make me theirs to keep. There were times when I felt bad about draining a man's finances. But all my dancer friends told me if it wasn't going to be me, then the next chick would get it and *if you don't want him, pass him to me.* They saw a repeat customer as consistent money and after that revelation, I began to see it the same way.

I grew tired of listening to the broken record about the same thing over and over again! Nonetheless, I had to suck it up and deal with it because he was paying me for my time.

CHAPTER 5

The Stripping Therapist

At *Flashdancers*, I met many lonely men who literally gave me everything they had to their names. I wore many hats at work. I was their therapist, their fantasy, and their friend. I was a shoulder to cry on or someone they could just kick it with, **no drama attached.** Whatever the need was, I could provide it. Work nights were like paid date nights. There wasn't a lot of financial consistency, but there was one thing I noticed; the stock market directly affected us. It was like the change in weather and I never knew what I was going to get.

Meet Alejandro, one of my clients from Queens, New York. Alejandro was a hedge fund analyst for a wealth management company, and one of the biggest closet freaks I'd encountered. I was impressed by his status within his professional life and shocked by his arousal for pain. When he came to the club, he became a subservient, fetish-driven trick. He wanted one of us girls to smack him across the face and tell him he was a piece of shit. Pain turned him on. He wanted me to ram my 6-inch stiletto heel into his balls and choke him. I'd take his belt, tie it around his neck, and walk him on all fours; like a dog.

Meet Gary Johnson, a nice guy from the midwest suburbs of Chicago who worked in the publishing industry. He came into the club one night with some co-workers for a farewell night out on the town. I was on stage when he noticed me. There was a rotation for stage dancing, so if you missed me on stage, you'd have to wait for me to go back on. *Flashdancers* was extremely busy and although it was smaller than most clubs, it was easy to lose someone in there. When people tipped the girls on stage, they normally gave $1 to $5 on average. Gary waited for me to go back up on stage, handed me $50 bill and said, "Please come see me when you're finished." It was so busy that night, I had a mental waitlist for table dances. I decided I wanted to see what this guy was about. The more someone was interested in you, the more you could get out of them...if you play your cards right.

Gary and I had a good time at the bar. Even though he was nearly 40, he was unmarried, and had no children, which to me was a red flag—Personally, I feel that if a person is single in their 40s and wants to be in a relationship, they should question and analyze why they're not connecting well with others—but he was a nice enough guy. The more we got to know each other, the more he fell in love with me. I was used to men having this reaction to me but I was still on the clock and time was money. In life, you have to communicate and explain the things you need and want. If Gary couldn't give me what I wanted, I needed to work. So I would simply ask to get paid for the time we hung out at the bar and if he didn't want to compensate me, I'd have to make my rounds on the floor table dancing. Gary understood this because he had previously dated a dancer at *Scores*.

In the beginning, this was an ideal situation for me. Whether you were a bartender, hostess, or dancer, we all wanted the same thing; a regular customer to come see us, pay us a shitload of money for hanging out and drinking. Who wouldn't want to get paid for hanging out and drinking?! For me, Gary was that customer. Every dancer's dream. A unicorn. I knew I would make at least $1,500 to $3,000 every time I saw him.

For a while, it was fun. We would laugh, drink, and share stories, both good and bad. I was making money just to hang out. Gary was determined to date me so he would come to the club often, about one to three times a week. As a result, he was spending large amounts of money in an attempt to make me fall in love with him.

My philosophy is, men are hunters. The hunt is more important than the kill. Once a guy dates a girl or sleeps with her, most times, he is onto the next. Why not play him for as long as you can and never give him what he wants? Play the player and in the end, YOU WIN!

But as time went by, Gary started getting frustrated with me. For about five years, I was able to string him along by feeding him the classic story that I'd been hurt before and was scared to date again. I truly felt bad about this part of my job. I'd often have to tell myself, *Leave the emotions at the door. You have a job to do*, but I knew Gary was a gold mine, and that if I didn't strike while the iron was hot, another dancer would gladly step in and complete the job I felt guilty about doing. So I sucked it up and continued to play the role. I said whatever I could to keep the money consistent.

But Gary wasn't getting what he wanted, and things went from fun to mentally draining. One day we'd be at the bar laughing and joking, the next we'd be arguing like an actual couple. I used to think I had a small impact on Gary's life, but I realized, he ruined his own life. And as it turned out, Gary wasn't being totally truthful with me either. During that time he was consistently coming to the club, I found out he also had a girl coming from Russia to live with him. They met online through an "international dating site". Gary wouldn't admit to it but I'm sure it was something similar to a mail-order bride service. Over time, she sensed something was off with Gary. He told me bits and pieces about the situation, but I didn't pry or ask too many questions I wasn't trying to get involved. My only goal was to get as much of his money as I possibly could. But Gary was forcing the issue by professing his love for me. He began having issues at work, and with his Russian female friend, who sensed that something was off—because of his feelings for me, he said, he wasn't emotionally or financially available to her. I felt bad. Clearly, in chasing the idea of he and I being an actual couple, he was allowing his own life to slip away. At the same time, I didn't want to let go of the easy and consistent money that came with the situation. But Gary was beginning to be more than I wanted to handle.

One night, Gary came into *Flashdancers* as he always did. We sat at the bar. The bar at *Flashdancers* was u-shaped with a sushi bar attached. Yes, they served actual sushi. Needless to say, the strip club with a sushi counter generated a lot of bad jokes. But it was nice to be able to have a California roll if I wanted one. We had dinner there quite frequently. On this particular night, Gary didn't want to eat. He had an upset look on his face and didn't want to talk much either. All he wanted to do was complain about the way things were. He said I was difficult and he didn't understand why we couldn't be together. He mentioned the psychic he'd gone to seek clarity from, who had advised him to keep pursuing me because eventually, I'd come around. (Whoever this psychic was, she had really done me a solid.) Soon it exploded into drama; visible drama for everyone to see. I don't care to be a spectacle or a sideshow, but we got into an argument and both of us lost our tempers. In the end, I was yelling at him, telling him to leave because he had issues and I was done. He replied by saying he had looked up my "symptoms" and I had a borderline personality disorder. To be honest, neither one of us was working with a full deck. I clapped my hands to applaud his dramatic scene and dismissed him.

Of course, it kept going. Until one day, I woke up with a guilty conscience. I decided it was time to let Gary go. I felt bad for draining his accounts, knowing I couldn't give him what he wanted. When he got to the club, he sat down and ordered a Corona. He always started his night off with a beer. He meticulously squeezed the lime into the beer bottle, then he moved on to the chilled shots of Patrón. I ordered a dirty Belvedere Martini. As I sat there with Gary, I told him that our relationship wasn't working. I told him that maybe he should move on. I was calm I didn't want to argue with him. After I spoke my piece, I got up and left the bar. I thought he might get upset and storm out. But later on, I found out he paid one of the other girls to hang out with him. That made my blood **boil**. I was upset with him. But it proved the old saying, "If you don't get the money, the next girl will." I decided to take his ass to the cleaners after I heard that.

It was game on! Eventually, Gary stopped coming to the club.

Some years had passed and I needed to get my *black book* clientele list back in order, so I reached out to him. He was always consistent, and that's what I was looking for. As it turned out things between him and his Russian friend had gone from bad to worse. Apparently the Russian felt so alienated by his obsession with dancers that *she* had become one herself. She ended up having an affair and getting pregnant. The baby, Gary found out, was not his.

Another regular I had, Mitch Biel, an ironworker from Queens, was also in his late 40s and living with his mom. He wasn't the coolest guy around and didn't have many friends. He was a storyteller and clearly had issues. In social settings where fantasy rules, people tell stories all the time. Most of the time you can filter what's real or not real but this guy had more stories than Dr. Seuss! He seemed nice and sweet in the beginning; **they all do.** Something about him was off. Again, I don't judge but I was a little weirded out with this one at times. As a dancer, I always worried about my safety and always wondered if anyone was following or stalking me. Sometimes it comes with the territory. So if there was ever a customer I was worried about, *he* was the one!

Mitch would tell me stories about his "ex-girlfriend" who was a dancer as well. I'm sure they were only actually dating in his mind. In this world, some guys have a perception of us as their girlfriends without ever going on a date or without the commitment of a relationship. I took everything they said with a grain of salt. He would tell me how she cleaned him out when he had a big lawsuit settlement. I was a listening ear and of course, it was therapeutic for him to have someone to vent to. But at the same time, I was thinking to myself, *Damn...why didn't I meet him when he had all that settlement money?* This customer was another clingy and emotionally needy man who fell in love with me. I seemed to always attract men with "mommy issues". It's funny because I was always the "mommy" of the group of my friends since I was always nurturing with maternal instincts.

Like so many of us, he had family issues he needed to get off his chest. He always vented and complained about his family, which was fine because I was there to listen and console. One thing I got annoyed with was when the customer complained about a problem and never did anything about it. I grew tired of listening to the broken record about the same thing over and over again! Nonetheless, I had to suck it up and deal with it because he was paying me for my time. Mitch once told me a story about his "ex-girlfriend" stabbing him. He showed me the huge scar it left behind and it made me feel sympathy for him. But when he would stress me out, I started to understand why she might have stabbed him. Shit, I had thoughts of stabbing him from time to time. I was losing my patience and the money couldn't compensate for the therapy sessions I had to endure. I wasn't a licensed therapist and he desperately needed to see one.

Unlike many of the girls I worked with over the years, I wasn't willing to do just anything for a buck. Dancers like me, who hustled for our money, frowned upon "dirty girls" the prostitutes and half-hookers who would go the extra mile with sexual favors. We didn't allow them into our circles because we had no respect for them and they had no respect for the game.

CHAPTER 6

Easy Money

Living the fast life at such an early age brought on addictions of my own. While dancing at *Flashdancers* I picked up a nasty cocaine habit that was introduced to me by my friend Chad, who had a huge drug problem. Since then, I have always questioned how much of a friend he really was. Friends shouldn't give friends drugs to try, that's a big no-no. A part of me wanted to die. I was truly flirting with death. I did stupid things, endangering myself and others. Sometimes I'd drive drunk knowing the harmful effects. My substance abuse was definitely clouding my judgment. My environment and the people in it were crazy. Maybe I was becoming a product of that. Aside from the actual drugs and alcohol I was consuming, I was also addicted to money. This was the hardest habit of them all to kick. No amount was ever enough. Shopping was instant gratification for me. I developed extreme shopping habits, buying overly expensive items like $5,000 Chanel Bags and $1,500 Christian Louboutin shoes. I didn't even immediately wear some of the things I bought. I just purchased them because I *could*. Being able to do these things stroked my ego. Coming from very little, I was in awe at what I could purchase with my own money.

Since the rules at *Flashdancers* were so strict, I needed to find a way to work less without having to pay fines since I slipped into a depression and drank heavily. There were times I drank so much that I couldn't work. I'd be stuck in the bathroom paralyzed in fear. I was disappointed in myself for allowing depression to go this far without doing something about it sooner. I didn't know exactly what to do next, but I knew I needed to make a change. *Flashdancers* had a good reputation and because of its location, the financial flow was steady. But as years passed I started to chafe under the many rules put in place by the owner of the club, Eric, who kept dancers on a strict schedule that made it impossible to have any freedom. I felt like a slave to my job. In the end, it wasn't a lack of money that made me unhappy working there, but the feeling of being locked down. I came to the conclusion that everything has an expiration date, and I stayed at *Flashdancers* way past mine. I had to leave. One thing I've learned about being in unhappy situations is if you don't change your environment, then it will get the best of you.

The strip club industry was a small world and you'll find yourself seeing the same faces in different clubs. During my transition phase, I ran into my friend Claudia, who I met while working at *Flashdancers.* She'd left and was working at a place called *Hustlers.* She said she was making crazy money *and* working her own schedule. I was scared to move on to other clubs—I'd heard about the sex and raunchy things going on at other places. I mean how could I compete with that? Claudia assured me I didn't have to do anything I didn't want to and I would still be able to make money. I didn't tell Eric I was going to *Hustlers.* He was notorious for not allowing girls to come back to his club after working at other places. So if you left and got caught, there goes your steady income. I decided to try it out and hoped one of his spies didn't catch me. Exploring other options was a breath of fresh air for me. Much later, I was happy to read in the papers that a group of dancers had decided to turn the tables on Eric and sued *Flashdancers* and other clubs for overtime. They ended up reaching a

$4.3 million-dollar settlement. I was happy they had the courage to stand up to him. I didn't have it in me at the time.

I did well at *Hustlers*, and you could tell from the way I looked. At the time, I was driving a Mercedes and carried a Gucci handbag. I liked to stand out. This wasn't such a good thing in Brooklyn, where I had moved into an apartment complex in what turned out to be a not-very-good neighborhood. There were always meth heads hanging around, and it turned out some of them were watching. One night after returning home from a barbeque, the doorbell rang. My roommate at the time answered and saw two guys with clipboards. They were white guys, in their fifties, and looked like maintenance men, so he unlatched the door, only to find himself pistol-whipped in the face. As it turned out, underneath the clipboards the guys were concealing guns. They forced their way into the apartment and demanded to know the combination to the safe where my money and jewelry were kept. "No, fuck that shit," I said, as the guy jammed his gun into my spine. Looking back, it was crazy to do. I'd been drinking but I wasn't drunk. I was more shocked someone had the nerve to bust up in my spot like that. I could tell the guys were nervous, like it was their first time, which made what I said next even crazier: "You are going to shoot me? Go fuck yourself!" They ended up carrying the safe out of the apartment. I don't know if they ever got it open. I could never figure out who sent these people but that incident was the end of my urban experiment. I may have been stubborn and fearless in the moment, but in the end, I cared about my own life enough to move from New York City to the suburbs. I wanted to be in close proximity of people who had their *own* money and could afford nice things. I didn't want anyone paying that much attention to me or my belongings. I felt safer and with my lifestyle being what it was, safety mattered.

When you're in the strip club business, you succumb to the lifestyle easily. You begin to believe making a grand a night is ordinary. By now, I'm about 24-years-old, considered a veteran, and working at my third strip club, *Hustlers*. My name at *Hustlers* was Akira, which I picked from a baby book the House Mom gave me. Every club I worked at had a different dynamic. At *Lace* and *Flashdancers*, it was every woman for herself. *Hustlers* had more of a team environment. The dancers worked in packs, kind of like the animals you'd see on the Discovery Channel. Two or three bodies were better than one. When choosing your team, you wanted girls who carried their own weight and who you trusted to call you when the money came in. At *Flashdancers*, I had been a top earner. But at *Hustlers*, I started at the bottom. In order to not leave the club in the negative, I needed to befriend the right girls and learn the dynamic amongst the team. I quickly noticed that Claudia, Camile, and Casey were the top earners, and I was desperate to learn how they kept customers in the Champagne rooms for hours and why Lorenzo, the host, always called them for his clients' needs.

Lorenzo is an Italian guy from Brooklyn with a heavy New York accent. He was one of the four hosts whose job was to place the customer with a girl or girls that could keep his attention for as long as possible. I needed to get on Lorenzo's good side. The strip club business is a whole world with its own hierarchy, rules, customs, and believe it or not, morals and principles. As you know by now, I had my own morals and principles. Unlike many of the girls I worked with over the years, I wasn't willing to do just anything for a buck. Dancers like me, who hustled for our money, frowned upon "dirty girls" the prostitutes and half-hookers who would go the extra mile with sexual favors. We didn't allow them into our circles because we had no respect for them and they had no respect for the game.

They didn't know how to work a custy's emotions or their pockets. They were lowering the bar, making it harder for us to make good money and poisoning the playing field. I saw it happen all too often: A good solid regular custy would get paired with a "dirty girl". He'd get a blowjob or sex and after that, he'd be tainted. Ruined. Because now when he comes back, he's looking for the same experience. Before, I could've gotten five hours worth of money out of him without having to give anything up. Now I might be able to get an hour before he's bored and goes on the hunt for *that* chick. It's like a dog that stops eating its healthy food after getting a taste of bacon.

The dirty girls pissed me off, but I also felt bad for them. I knew somewhere along the way, they'd lost their confidence and sense of self. They could have easily been doing what I was doing; getting the money and keeping their knees together. But they punked out, letting a customer offer them money *only* in exchange for some sort of sexual favor. At certain points, I tried to mother hen some of these girls by teaching them the tricks I had learned to get what they needed without losing their self-respect. Our job was to provide the fantasy. That's what kept the customer coming back. Quite frankly, you can make the money without having to be a slut. What I came to know is that a lot of these women had been violated and hurt inside, so they were numb. **I get it.**

We always knew who was hooking based on the clientele they would go in private rooms with and/or the hosts they worked with. In this type of work environment, you need to know what role everyone plays, what titles each person holds, who to stay away from and who to be nice to. You have to know the importance of each player. The hosts were kind of like pimps in the strip club. They had direct access to the clients and their job was to keep them happy by sending them girls they thought they'd like. In exchange, the dancers had to tip the hosts a percentage of their earnings. In the meantime, the hosts were also getting a tip from the client. So in retrospect, they were raking in the money. The host could be either your best friend or worst enemy. Like the girls, there were clean hosts and there were dirty hosts. Now, there were girls who outright had sex in the club and the host knew it. The hosts also knew who wasn't giving it up in the club. Based on that information, each host would match a client with a dancer that fit their needs.

Lorenzo was a clean host. He was cool as shit and he ran the show; very Hugh Hefner-like. If you were a dancer, you wanted to play nice with Lorenzo, because he could help you make money. Lorenzo always liked me. I think he had a thing for Asian girls. Whenever I worked with him, he used to hook me up. He and I had a little arrangement in place. He would put me in a room with a client *knowing* that I wasn't their type, but I'd still make money off that client. Once the client decided I wasn't their type, Lorenzo would find them "the right girl". Whatever! It was all a scheme. Lorenzo would purposely milk the customer and I would slide him 20-30% of my earnings from that client for hooking me up. **Easy money.**

Once you worked with a host, you had to remain loyal to him. Otherwise, he wasn't hooking you up. You'd have to work for everything yourself. It was nice to get thrown into a room and collect $500- $1,000 per hour just because you were one of Lorenzo's girls. I looked up to the hosts admiring their power and connections. They pulled in more money than us and did less work. Watching them, I knew one day I wanted to be in that kind of powerful position. At one point, reading up on Heidi Fleiss's story, I was tempted to become a madame. Of course, I knew it was illegal. But in the clubs, where half of the women were hookers anyway, it started to seem like a feasible career move, and one that later on, I would get dangerously close to.

Hustlers was party central and customers were known for blowing lines. Supplying the cocaine wasn't required of course, but it was absolutely necessary if you wanted to keep a customer in your grasp. We had to be very careful about doing so because at any moment the club could be crawling with undercovers and drug-sniffing canines. I remember sitting in the dressing room and doing my makeup at the bench in front of the mirror with bright white vanity bulbs. The dog came in and walked directly up to me. My heart dropped and I thought, *Oh shit!* I calmed down quickly when I realized I didn't have anything on me. I was thinking to myself, *What does he smell?* After he sniffed me, he kept going. The dog sniffed each locker and stopped at one. The House Mom was ordered to open the locker and the police searched it for drugs. Nothing was found. But anyone of us could've easily gotten busted for possession. Luckily, it never happened. My guilty conscience made me panicky. The undercovers that came in posing as regular customers were easy to spot. They weren't so smooth with their questions. Dealing with so many men regularly, we learned to analyze their behaviors. Too many "out of the ordinary" questions was a red flag to us. As soon as one of us detected or suspected an undercover, we would let the other girls know. In some instances, we looked out for each other.

Unlike at *Flashdancers*, I had no schedule at *Hustlers* and I enjoyed the freedom. I was an independent contractor that worked whenever I wanted to for however long I wanted to work. Management didn't care as long as I made money, and I was making more money than I'd ever seen. The shopping habits that I'd developed working at *Flashdancers* started to become a full-blown addiction. It was all or nothing with me. I spent and spent until even that got boring and I no longer felt a rush when I did it. It was time for a new addiction. That's when things got really wild.

I met Camile through my friend Claudia, who had encouraged me to come from *Flashdancers to Hustlers.* They were the ones who showed me how *the game* really worked: And the way that it worked was drugs. Not for myself. For the customers. I had long stopped doing cocaine myself, but I started keeping it on me for the customer to use. That's what would keep them in the Champagne Room for hours and hours. The guys were usually grateful. Back then, when Howard Stern was talking about *Scores* on the radio and the strip club business in New York was doing well, everything was like a big party. Men would come into the club, snort some lines, and buy bottles. Custys just wanted to escape their everyday lives and be in the company of sexy women with no strings attached. We would order food from the diner, eat, chill, and talk. One of the customers might be rubbing a dancer's leg, another one is off in a corner telling his whole life story. Every night was different, but on a typical night, what we encountered was all in the name of fun. My clientele list, which was already large from my time at *Flashdancers*, grew even larger. I had over 30 sharks which was what we called, *Big Moneymakers*. One of my high rollers was the owner of a major sneaker company. Back then, the men who went to strip clubs in New York were *bosses* and had plenty of money to throw around. I loved it. I didn't have any customers with nasty or odd fetishes, although Camile did. But one thing that was definitely true was that many of them in high-power positions wanted to be submissive at the end of the day. I was in no position to judge them. I just wanted my money!

Before I left the scene to have my daughter and focus on my family, I'd been part of a little clique. I guess you could call us the Get Money Crew. *We made mad money and kept our circle tight. I was the only Asian girl. Aside from me, the girls were either Spanish or Caucasian. While ethnicity didn't matter to us dancers, it might've made a difference with the customers.*

CHAPTER 7

The Get Money Crew

The girls at the club were pretty gossipy. I didn't care for that. In my experience, gossip brings nothing but drama, problems, wars, and battles that could easily be stopped before they even start if everyone would mind their own damn business! It's not that difficult. Living in that world, I learned so much about people. I've learned that most people who gossip are usually unhappy with themselves. The negativity you spew about others is only a reflection of who you are. How could any of us judge when all of the girls had stories of insecurity, relationship problems, sexual abuse, poor childhoods, abandonment issues, complexes, mommy/daddy issues, and just overall shitty circumstances?

One day at work, while I was still the "new girl" at *Hustlers,* I noticed Mia in the dressing room. Mia was a Jewish girl from Queens who had an odd walk, she walked with a limp. She was very friendly and outgoing with everyone. There was a reason for this. Mia was a pawn. She was cool with everyone but she wasn't the type of girl to make money on her own. She didn't have her own clients and needed the help of others to make the money. The scoop on Mia was that her boyfriend was pimping her out and taking all her money, all while sleeping around on her. Everyone seemed to know this except Mia. I wasn't sure if it was because no one had the heart to tell her, or they chalked it up to being none of their business. All

I knew was that if these girls were "cool" with Mia to her face but talked about her behind her back, they would treat me the same way.

I'm certain that everyone at *Hustlers* thought I was a bitch. Cocky, arrogant, egotistical. To be fair, I was. That's how I gained my respect. I tried not to think about or get involved with the petty drama. Back when I was working at *Lace*, I'd let my personal life get all wrapped up with my professional life. In the city, I'd developed the belief that you shouldn't mix friendship with business. I had nothing in common with these women aside from the club. I had to keep my mentality in check so I didn't get caught up in all the dumb shit. If it didn't pay my bills, I had no vested interest in it. I'd tell myself, "You're here to make money, not friends".

Then there was Natalie. She was the younger sister of the madam of a massage parlor. She was also from Queens. I met Natalie one summer while I was at Camile's bachelorette party on the Jersey Shore. Camile and I were forming our crew, and she thought Natalie would be a good addition. I agreed. Natalie was young and cute and we needed a fresh face for our customers. Let me clarify what we meant by, *fresh face*. Guys always had more of a preference for the "girl next door" look, in other words, a girl that didn't look like a stripper. Girls that **didn't** have major cosmetic surgery done (i.e: the big injected lips and the big breast implants) were in high demand. Natural beauty is priceless and goes a long way.

The night I met the sneaker CEO, he was leaving the men's room at the club. He had a "surfer" look to him. He was 5'11," had sun-kissed skin, a muscular build, and long shaggy hair. I could tell he had money. He had swag, too. He was wearing a Christian Audiger hoodie, which was a several hundred dollar sweater; I knew that because I had a few of them myself. Not only was he wealthy, but he was also good looking with a great personality. Everyone loved this guy. He was definitely a *Hustlers* favorite. He only drank Johnny Walker Blue, sniffed blow all night, and partied like a rockstar without the guitar! He even gave us girls lap dances! This was the kind of guy that made me wonder, *What is a man like this doing hanging around a bunch of dancers? He can probably have any woman he wants.* Soon enough, I found out he was married and had a mistress in California. We've all heard that story before. We didn't care. The clients weren't the only ones that wanted no strings attached. We had our own lives and boyfriends to go home to. This customer was a big spender and us dancers just wanted his money. I was shocked he revealed his profession to me. I was able to get him to come in a good amount of times and he was a guaranteed $3,000 per visit. I did very well when he came in and was able to use him to help my girls profit off his wealth as well. Sometimes, he even took us shopping.

There were times when the club was so dead, a lot of us girls would text our clients and invite them to the club. We needed a "score." So if he was in town he would come to save the day for me and my girls! Our night went from being at a negative $300 to up $3-5,000 just like that! The stock market affected us dancers tremendously. I remember looking at the stock market numbers regularly to see how Wall Street did on any particular day. That was an indicator of how clients were feeling about possibly **sharing the wealth.**

As time went on, business in the strip club decreased tremendously. At this point, it was 2008. The economy was in trouble and so was the strip club business. Ninety-five percent of our customers were hard-partying Wall Street guys. We had other customers like tourists, bachelor parties, or a convention on any given weekend. But when the financial crisis hit and the suits stopped coming in, the strip club became a ghost town. Some nights, the number of dancers working surpassed the number of customers that came in. *Hustler* was starting to live up to its name. Men were being bombarded by money-hungry dancers the moment they walked in the door. That had never been my style. I always liked to wait until the guy had at least one drink in his system to loosen him up before I started my ***sophisticated hustle***. Now we had to hustle more and more to keep the money flowing. The competition was getting tougher and tougher. The stripping industry as we knew it was coming to an end.

It was right around that time that I got pregnant. Dating men when you're leading this kind of lifestyle can be very tricky. I had trust issues to begin with and working in a strip club didn't exactly make it better. Also, the simple truth is that a lot of men can't handle a woman involved in the stripping business. They get jealous. I can understand their frustration, but I never had any patience for that. If you can't take the heat, get out of the kitchen. What's worse is when they become controlling, or abusive. In the past, I'd been called a whore, a thot, or was accused of doing dirty things. I wouldn't tolerate the disrespect. I'm the wrong girl to attempt to control. I talk back. I do what I want and I don't ask for permission to make money, regardless of how it's made. This was my bread and butter, screw whoever didn't like it.

In the five years that we had been together, my boyfriend and I had had our ups and downs. But at the time, we were in a good place. Things were aligning (or so I thought). Plus, I was burned out. I was 25 years old, and I'd been in the industry for nearly a decade. I was beginning to feel like a scumbag, walking into my nice home in the 'burbs at the same time the regular folks were on their way to work. So I decided it was time to leave it all behind. To let go of my independence and allow him to be the primary breadwinner. It was a challenging decision for me but I passed my client list to my dancer friends. If someone was going to make money off my customers, I wanted it to be the dancers in my circle. I mean, why not? I hung up my dancing shoes and my then-boyfriend and I celebrated our five year anniversary by getting engaged. Our child would have a different kind of life than the one I had experienced, I thought. We were going to be the perfect family. Almost immediately, my boyfriend became an asshole and started sleeping around.

My daughter was my fourth pregnancy. Before, I was just never quite ready for motherhood. I had goals and having a baby wasn't at the top of my priority list. But I hated birth control, which had a negative psychological effect on me. Between the lifestyle I lived and my own suicidal thoughts, I didn't need more chemicals messing with my head. By the time I found out what my boyfriend was up to, I was three months pregnant. I called Planned Parenthood and asked what my options were and they referred me to other states that would provide abortions after three months. I was extremely upset and depressed. I had a terrible pregnancy. I had gestational diabetes and I was an emotional eater. I turned to food a lot because I was so depressed. I ate strawberry Haagen-Dazs ice cream as often as I could. I'd never been over 110 pounds and I was 160 pounds. I'd lost my sexy and wasn't getting the same attention I was used to receiving. I wasn't being loved at home either. People that once cared about me, seemed to forget I existed. The only thing that made me feel better was the ice cream and constant kicking coming from my baby, which, surprisingly, it turned out that I wanted after all. Some say the baby can't feel the mother's emotions while they're in the womb. I was afraid my baby would come out sad and depressed because of the way I felt when I was pregnant.

After I had my daughter, I was vulnerable and felt alone. But something told me, *you've got this.* I made a declaration to myself: *lose the baby weight, get back to work, make as much money as I can, get out, put a down payment on a house, and start a business.* Then I did exactly that. I hired a fitness trainer for myself and a nanny for my daughter. I got back in shape, regained my confidence, dusted off my heels, and went back to the club. Before you judge me let me explain that my ONLY motive was to take care of my family. I'm not against punching a clock and earning a paper check. I needed financial freedom, and this was the quickest way I knew how to get it. By no means did I want to make dancing a lifetime career. I was a **Mommy by day and Madam at night**. I would come home from work and go to bed at 6 am. I would get up at 11 am, get my daughter to preschool by Noon and then take my nanny home. While my daughter was at school I would run errands or nap, then pick her up by 3 pm. My time with her was so precious. She was such a happy baby and she had this amazing, unique laugh that just made everyone smile. Her smile and laugh was magical! After school, I enjoyed taking her out a lot; our favorite thing to do was going to the park. My goal in life as a Mom is to create memories with my daughter. Toys get played with, then tossed to the side and then eventually donated to The Salvation Army. But my theory is creating happy and special memories can never be taken away; those moments will stay with you forever. My nanny would come to my house around 7 pm and this is when I would get ready to go to work. I would shower and get dressed. Getting dressed for work felt good; **I finally felt like a Boss.** I would dress in black slacks, a white blouse and a black blazer with my black patent leather red bottoms. No longer was I going to work in sweatsuits and leggings; to put on 6-inch stilettos and a sexy dress. I was going to work in business attire and it felt amazing. I finally felt accomplished and proud of myself for making it so far and coming a long way.

I really felt like a businesswoman and the boss of my own company. When my neighbors and friends would ask me what I did, I told them I owned a Modeling Agency in the city. I was in the process of starting my agency, but instead, I decided to do a consignment business. Camile and I not only made money from cash and checks. We also dabbled with some shopping with the customer's permission of course. We had a hook up at Saks Fifth Avenue in Manhattan and the girl would put the guy's card on file for purchases when she got into work she would run the credit card. We didn't want to spend our own money if we didn't have to. It was nice but eventually, I just wanted the money. I mean how many bags, shoes, and watches did a girl need? We always split everything up evenly. I would accept the gifts and look to flip the merchandise for cash instead. Not only was I trying to make money with selling the gifted high ticket items but I wanted to get a mobile credit card terminal to run our own transactions at the club.

A mobile credit card terminal was necessary for some of the work we did outside the club. Sometimes we couldn't get the customer out of his hotel room. Most guys had a room upstairs from the hotel bar we were at and would like to go up "to party". We would go there to drink and hang, then try to get them in the club. The guy was in heaven; 4 or 5 hot girls in his hotel room. This was a challenge to get him out. But then a lightbulb went off in our heads... why not just charge the guys ourselves and forget the clubs getting their cut (more money for us). This is where the credit card terminals would come in handy. Our operation was expanding, we were operating both out of hotel rooms and multiple gentlemen's club. Everyone wanted a piece of the pie. Everyone wanted to jump on the **Money Train.**

When we went fishing at upscale bars, steakhouses, and restaurants, I was usually the driver and I drove a 2010 White Escalade with black leather interior. Camile, my partner in crime would be in the front passenger seat either booking hotel rooms or calling/texting the host to get the Champagne Room ready. The girls would be in the back entertaining the guy or shoving their boobs in his face and/or bumps of cocaine up his nose. My truck was big but I refused to take the baby seat out. If you're a Mom, you know taking that car seat in and out is a pain in the butt. I could never get it strapped as tight as my child's father did, so I just left it for safety reasons. I had the two captains chair in the middle and the full seat that would fit 3 in the back. I can fit about 5 people in my truck but if we really needed the 6th chair one of the girls would sit in the car seat. My truck was a personal and work vehicle. At night there was a car service for the girls and customers. I'd have to clean the truck in the morning because sometimes cocaine got on the baby seat and drinks were left behind in the cup holders. In the daytime, it was my Mommy Mobile with a drop-down screen that was attached into the roof. I would play *Baby Einstein* and *Elmo Sing-Alongs* for my daughter. She would be sitting there with her two pigtails and baby bottle watching the TV screen as I was making phone calls with Camile.

Work never stopped for us in the daytime. Camile would call me and I would have to deal with a dispute. I would be on the phone arguing with the customer and the credit card company. No one had to deal with this except Camile and I, but mostly me. I knew how to speak on a professional level and try to keep my composure. I remember being at my friend's pool with her kids and my daughter. She was looking at me crazy because the ugly in me came out when I had to deal with work and money stuff. The stress levels were through the roof. There were times I didn't want to answer Camile so I could just enjoy time with my daughter, but I had no choice. It was our bread and butter that depended on winning these chargebacks and it was worth anywhere from $5-10K per person. So I had to suck it up for the whole team and deal with the calls when they came. These were just the cards life dealt me and I did what I had to do because losing wasn't an option. Since then, that's been my attitude about life; no matter what comes my way, **I've got this.** For the next two years, I basically raised my daughter independently.

Although my goal had been to get in and get out, the money was never enough. Every time I reached my goal, I'd stay for just a little bit more. Money is like drugs, there's never enough. The difference between the two is, you can let go of the drugs but to live, you *always* need the money. The average price of a decent home in New York was between $300-500K, and it takes money to build a business. I had to keep that in mind and needed to make sure we were covered. It was taking longer than I wanted it to. In the past, I'd heard that it was frowned upon to still be stripping at 30, so it was embedded in my brain to get out before I hit that marker. Now I was 27; not only my own goals but the times had changed.

Before I left the scene to have my daughter and focus on my family, I'd been part of a little clique. I guess you could call us the **Get Money Crew**. We made mad money and kept our circle tight. I was the only Asian girl. Aside from me, the girls were either Spanish or Caucasian. While ethnicity didn't matter to us dancers, it might've made a difference with the customers. For example, a customer might have a preference of Asian girls, or Spanish chicks, or short girls, fat asses, big boobs, dark hair, etc. So we tried to be diverse. We weren't the only "clique" in the club. All of us were small organizations within the organization. The way it worked was, when one of us in the clique saw an opportunity for the other to make money, she would let you know. She would scratch your back and when the tables turned, you did the same for her. We helped one another, that's also how we became friends. When I came back to *Hustlers* after my hiatus, when my daughter was nine months old, I found out that the girls I had been working with had jumped ship. Supposedly there was some drama with Camile and Lorenzo. There was always politics at the clubs. Camile and Lorenzo ran *Hustlers* and if you messed with them, they would blacklist you. Apparently, Camile got my girls fired from *Hustlers.* So now they were all working at *Sapphire's* in Upper Manhattan. *Sapphire's, which* was in the original *Scores* location, is the club Howard Stern made famous. They even named a Champagne Room after him. The girls met big money guys there, and so that's where I went, too.

It was a difficult transition. I was learning the ropes all over again, and getting to know who's who. Every club had a different dynamic, you just had to learn it and go with the flow. What made it more difficult was that the "friends" I'd given my client list to were being shady with me. They wouldn't give my customers back. I was confused. Why were they treating me like an outsider; as if I hadn't done the noble gesture of greasing their palms before I left? *You gotta be kidding me.* Everything that happened thereafter was a chain reaction. Nothing occurred overnight.

The customers would be so drunk and doped up that they couldn't remember the night. I understood their pain. I've been there, out in the club popping bottles and have a $1,500 tab at the end of the night. I'm left sitting there like, What the fuck*? So, I felt their pain. However, their credit card troubles weren't my problem.*

CHAPTER 8

Buyer's Remorse

Times had changed. Good conversation and an occasional table dance were no longer enough. Everything I said and did mattered. It could have been the difference between getting a big check or wasting my time and going home with absolutely nothing at the end of the night. There were many nights I worked a full shift and went home with nothing. The one thing that hadn't changed was the presence of cocaine. Most of the guys who came into the club were drinking and doing drugs simultaneously, and coke was still the drug of choice for dancers to keep on hand. But everyone reacts differently. Usually, you got one of the two outcomes: aggressive or relaxed. Needless to say, we preferred our custys relaxed.

Meet my superstar, Molly. She was a fierce co-host when we entertained the custys. The men used drugs while they drank causing them to get *limp dick*. Their penis' couldn't get hard and truthfully that was fine with me because the girls weren't there to perform sexual favors anyway. On the flip side, when the guy couldn't get hard they would get frustrated and wanted to leave. If they left, the night was over! But I had a solution to that problem which would buy us more time. Molly had a way of milking the clock. **Who the hell is Molly?** MDMA aka "Molly" is ecstasy in a powder form. There are several ways to use the powder by putting it on your tongue, swallow a capsule and mix it in a drink, or you can sniff it. Within minutes, the custy was ready to party for hours! Also, my partner and I were taking a prescribed drug called Valium. Valium is a small blue pill with the letter "V" on it, meant for anxiety. That pill was magic for us girls. There were times we'd be frustrated due to the stressful situation of trying to keep the money in-house, so we'd take Valium and the customer always thought the small blue pill was Viagra to help when they had trouble getting hard. Honestly, I took the Valium to keep me from choking someone out. When the customer took the pill, not only would this buy us more time but it would keep them calm in a relaxed state. No one wanted to deal with a horny and hyper guy!

Meet Barron, the CFO for a major hedge fund in Midtown Manhattan. Talk about a high roller. This guy would spend $100,000 every time he came in! He wanted to dance to a certain artist or song and sniff cocaine all night long. This guy was a dream come true. We didn't have guys like that at *Hustlers*. When he walked in the door, every girl in our crew made $10,000 minimum. We used crushed up Molly and mixed it in his cocaine. No table dances, no dirtiness, no drama…just pure fun!!!

We began to consistently mix Molly in the customer's cocaine and swiping their credit cards for every cent possible. Milking the time was important because when we swiped the card, the time stamps had to match up, otherwise, the customer could dispute the charge and win. Amex, in particular, had a reputation of siding with its customers. But when the clubs had video footage of the customers walking in, hourly swipes, and the customers walking out, who could argue? For his part, Barron never disputed a charge. His money was always good.

It was nice to make a $10,000 in one night and know that the money would clear. The feeling was so great that it put me on a high horse. We were the *it girls* and our crew ran shit. When we made money for the club, there were perks. There were things we could get away with that the other dancers didn't. We always got first pick of the schedule. Everyone had to work one weekend day and that was every dancer's nightmare because most of the Wall Street guys were at home on the weekends doing the family thing. The only traffic we got on the weekends would be the *bridge and tunnel* crowd. Bridge and tunnel was our nickname for the young customers that would have to cross a bridge and tunnel to get to the city like guys from Jersey, Long Island, and Westchester. No offense but those were the ones that didn't have big money to blow, usually having a budget of $100-200 max. All the big money was to be made during the week, after work with the customers that had business accounts and took clients out to show them a good time. If there was a high roller coming in the club, the host gave us first dibs on making that money.

But all good things must come to an end. Including my friendship with the girls from *Sapphire's.* Our falling-out had to do with my recurring depression. I'd been diagnosed with bipolar disorder and chose not to take the medication. Anything could trigger the depression, and when that happened I opted to stay home instead of going to work. Honestly, it was for everyone's own good. It was our job to spread happiness and if I wasn't feeling it, how was I to make any money? No one wants to be around Negative Nancy. But according to the Queen Bee of the group, who was very bossy and controlling, when I would stay home because of the depression, that meant I wasn't being supportive, because I wasn't there to help them make money. Once she said that, the rest of the group fell in line. That was how it always worked: If someone had beef with one of the main girls, the rest followed.

I wasn't a follower. And as I mentioned before, I wasn't in the game to make friends. Now I was disappointed and pissed off at myself because somehow it had happened anyway. I finally realized that making friends with these girls was a big mistake. My friendships with them hadn't been genuine. They were only friends with me because I could help them make money.

After that, I wouldn't mix money and friendships anymore. Not here. I never liked feeling like I needed someone, anyway. I was also a money maker and I knew how to work independently due to my time at *Flashdancers*. Thankfully, I was versatile and able to adapt to my environment and surroundings, easily. The definition of a ***sophisticated hustler.***

When you stay in disrespectful situations, things only get worse. It can be any kind of relationship: a friendship, a romantic relationship, or a professional relationship. In this case, it was a friendship and a professional relationship combined. So I left and went back to *Hustler* I was determined to figure shit out on my own.

By now, it's Fall 2011. I'm back at *Hustler*, using the same stage name, Akira, I had before I was pregnant. Everything was the way I remembered it. Camile was still the main girl, but her role changed. She was no longer a dancer, but a dancer turned licensed masseuse. Some clubs hired a female masseuse to enhance the customer's experience with actual back and shoulder rubs. In addition, Camile was working with a partner, Michelle. They were a packaged deal. This meant things got split three ways and no offense to Michelle, but she had never been a dancer and didn't have a client list because she was strictly a masseuse. She was really a sweetheart, but honestly, I didn't feel like Michelle had anything to bring to the table and I didn't want to split the money with more people than I had to. My opinion about splitting the money with Michelle made a light go off in Camile's mind, but it also caused turmoil in their friendship because eventually, Camile began to decrease Michelle's pay. That wasn't my problem. I wasn't there to make friends. I was there to make money and go home. The strip club business is very cut-throat and over the years, I'd learned that this business is a rat race; who could get to the money the fastest was all that mattered. At the beginning of my tenure as a dancer, I was nice and didn't want to take the other dancers' customers. I was polite about how I made my money, careful not to step on anyone's toes. But several years in, I became ruthless and knew I had to worry about myself. Strip clubs are a revolving door; customers and dancers came and went. I saw it all the time. So if the opportunity to make a decent amount of money presented itself, so be it. None of the girls nor the customers were a part of my real life, outside the club. My cut of the money was always my biggest concern so if I made my money off someone else's customer, **tough**. They'd do the same to me if I ever gave them the chance. If I had to expose a chick who wasn't pulling her weight, oh well! I wasn't going to let another broad fuck with my cut if she wasn't doing her part. **Period.**

There are plenty of women who are in the position I was in. Most people buy into the lie that stripping equates to hooking. They are **not** one in the same, there *is* a difference. For the sake of clarity, **I wasn't a prostitute.** I **never** had sex in exchange for money. We provided a good time for the customer and they paid for the entertainment. If I was sleeping with these men, I would have never needed to drug them, thus never being charged and arrested. Of course, some men were willing to pay us big money to sleep with them. Instead of prostituting, we showed many of them the time of their lives by drinking, drugging and swiping the hell out their credit cards. Some guys said they "wanted to get fucked," well they certainly got fucked, but not in the way they imagined.

You never knew what you were going to get from a person.

I discovered that every situation and every customer was different. Being a critical thinker was important. I had to make snap decisions. When you're partying, time flies. An hour passed quicker than the speed of light and before you knew it, we'd be in a Champagne Room with a customer for five or six hours, sometimes longer. If the money was good enough, there were times when the club would stay open past the 4 am closing time just for us. Every customer wasn't cool to be around. Some of them were downright annoying but we knew we would get big money out of them. Some of them were so fucking aggravating so Camile would give the customer a bump of "K," which was a cat tranquilizer known as Ketamine. This drug was sniffed and would put them in a blackout state of mind that we called a "K hole." Of course, it wouldn't kill the customer but they would be in a trance for a long period of time. Giving a customer a bump of Ketamine was the drug of choice among the girls. I could never understand taking a downer while you're out having fun. But to each his own. Ketamine was our saving grace from the customer who may have been aggressive or downright annoying. Once we gave it to them, that's it. It was lights out.

Looking back, we shouldn't have been dispensing drugs to these men because I wasn't entirely sure what effects the drug would have on each person. I never used the drug myself so I couldn't attest to how they could have reacted. Ketamine wasn't my department, however, watching the reaction of my co-workers and customers who used the drug, taught me the ropes. I had more experience with Molly and cocaine so I knew what dosages to give and what kind of high a person would have. The only remedies were either to let the drug wear off or to drink orange juice. Something about the acidic element of orange juice immediately snapped them out of the trance. I know it sounds crazy but based on the customer's level of tolerance, we knew who to give a specific drug to. The activities I chose to be involved in are unbelievable, even to me, and I'm glad no one ever overdosed on our watch because it was never my aim to harm anyone. I got caught up in bad situations as a result of my poor decisions, and everything subsequently became the norm. The lifestyle was just like any other addiction; I built a tolerance for it.

Once the customer was in a drug-induced state, we would run his credit card every hour on the hour. We milked him for everything we could. When we couldn't run the card any longer, we would give the customer orange juice, let him come to, and send him on his way. If the customer tried to dispute the charge, it was almost impossible for them to win their dispute. Every customer was seen on camera coming in and out of the strip club. What else is there to say? How can you explain that? The customers would be so drunk and doped up that they couldn't remember the night. I understood their pain. I've been there, out in the club popping bottles and have a $1,500 tab at the end of the night. I'm left sitting there like, *What the fuck*? So, I felt their pain. However, their credit card troubles weren't my problem. **Buyer's remorse**. There was also a flip side to the game. Once they tricked every dollar possible on us, they never came back. We could only do *that* for so long. Eventually, the club became quiet...dead. The only ones making money now were the ones suckin' and fuckin' for peanuts. Truthfully, I made more money just dancing. But once again, the game changed, so I changed the game.

If the guys smelled lying then it was game over. I always played the damsel in distress role; most of the time saying something like, "I had a stressful day at work and wanted to blow off some steam." That's the story I had to sell and men would buy it.

CHAPTER 9

Time To Go Fishing

Hustlers was becoming a ghost town and girls were actually giving sexual favors in exchange for $50. Desperate times called for desperate measures, but some shit just wasn't going to work for me.

Didn't they know they could make more for doing less?! What happened to this place?! I was so spoiled. I used to get paid thousands a night to hang, chill, and talk. I was determined to get what I wanted without having to degrade myself. I loved myself and I knew I had one thing those girls didn't, "the gift of gab". You see, being an entertainer at a strip club isn't just a pretty face and a nice body. These men wanted to engage in stimulating conversation. They wanted beauty and brains. This was like a game for me at work. Try to make the most money without having to do things I didn't want to do. These men were hustlers themselves; we're talking CFOs, CEOs, and Wall Street hedge fund guys. When I pictured Wall Street guys, I thought of that movie called "The Boiler Room." I thought of arrogant, cocky, pricks. But truthfully, some of the customers were okay guys, not all of them were assholes. I had some time to sit back and analyze my options. One day, a lightbulb went off! If the clients weren't coming in, then I'll bring them to us. At this point, I had nothing to lose. I was leaving negative $300 anyway, from paying the house fee, DJ, and house mom. I refused to go back to *Flashdancers* or *Sapphire's*. I strongly believe in the saying "Once you close that door, don't open it back up." I didn't need anyone. I was a strong woman who could figure things out on my own.

People gravitate towards me naturally. I never had a shortage of associates from all walks of life. I can network with the best of them. I'm outgoing and can frequently spot an opportunity with ease. Dancing was no longer my thing. I grew out of it and moved on to the managerial side. With the club being relatively empty, we had to find a way to bring the money to us. That's when I began *fishing*.

Fishing was a new client acquisition method I mastered. It meant going to bars and steakhouses looking for clients to bring back to the strip club. Like a fisherman or in this case, fisherwoman, I spent my time at sea hoping a big fish would take the bait. But this kind of fishing was way more complex than fishing at sea. The art of fishing meant dressing, acting and talking the part. With this new system of attracting new clients by frequenting bars and restaurants, I was no longer competing with dancers at the club. I was competing with escorts and hookers; plus I had to watch the bartenders, hosts, and waiters who were keeping an eye out for girls who were soliciting at their establishments. They wanted to keep their customers there for as long as they could. I was able to keep them away from me because I kept the persona of a customer by spending a lot of money. When I was out on fishing expeditions to bring men back to the clubs, I never felt bad about it. These men were dogs, to put it mildly. Most times, the men would approach me in public and that's how I'd hook them. Sometimes I'd send them a shot and hook them that way.

I'd meet men at cigar bars, hotel bars, and restaurant bars. I would go to these establishments dressed up in slacks and a blazer; keeping a very natural, everyday look. If I'd done any kind of noticeable cosmetic surgery, it would've been a dead giveaway. I had to look the part, practice my story, and stick to it. My name was Akira at *Hustlers*, so I used the same name when I was out fishing. Only this time I wasn't dancing. I was Akira, the consignment shop owner who also did marketing and promotions for restaurant groups. I made business cards with the legit information of my company and a separate cell phone for work. I had to be precise because there was a small window of time between 5 pm and 9 pm to grab some guys. Fishing any time after 9 pm would leave me shit out of luck because the "after work" crowd would be winding down. I'd sit alone, pretending I was waiting on someone. Often times, the men would come over and ask questions; *what's your name, where are you from, where do you work,* etc. Thank goodness I'm outgoing and witty at the same damn time. I had to answer quick and fast on the fly. If the guys smelled lying then it was **game over.** I always played the damsel in distress role; most of the time saying something like, "I had a stressful day at work and wanted to blow off some steam". That's the story I had to sell and men would buy it. They wanted to be the reason my day ended better than it started. While they were asking questions about me, I also had some questions for them. Before I would continue talking to the guy, I was careful not to keep the company of too many men. I didn't want to get flagged as a hooker or escort. If I was labeled as either, I wouldn't have been able to come back to that place and fish. I used a filtering process to size a guy up by his attire; shoes and watch. I was a watch girl and I knew my watches very well. I had an eye for material things and knew the value of the watches and shoes the men wore. My theory with this is: if a guy can spend $100,000 on a watch then he had the money to throw my way and more than likely wouldn't mind balling on a night out with a hot girl.

When fishing, not only would I have to dress and act the part, but I had to do some research. I had to find out where the guys with finance jobs hung out. Once I knew which places were their top spots, I'd scope out the crowd looking for the high rollers. There's an art to it. I'd open my tab at the bar and check for the types of cards being used at the bar for other open tabs. Sometimes I'd be close enough to the card to peep the name and google the holder to see what kind of position they held at a company. I also had an eye for credit cards; which cards had higher limits and which ones had no limits at all. The watch, shoes, and credit card type were all indicators of a *high roller.* Once I hooked the guy, they followed me wherever I went. I would do shots with them and suggest going to a strip club. What man is going to turn that down? I pretended I'd never been to a strip club before, that it was my first time, and told them that I liked girls. I was a great actress. Who knows, maybe one day I'll pursue my dream of acting...but I digress. Once I was done with the filtering process, I'd call Camile and Michelle to help with the client once we arrived at the club. We'd go to *Hustlers*, I'd walk in with the customer, and retrieve the credit card and ID from them for Lorenzo to run. In my eyes, I was the hero coming to save everyone's pockets by providing an opportunity for everyone to make money. I did *very* well working alone. I liked things done a certain way and in this new line of work I would like to call Club Promoting and Hosting, there were no "do-overs." Everything I said and did was calculated. If I misstepped, the guy would leave and there goes the night. Due to that critical fact, I preferred to fish alone.

Since I was working back at *Hustlers* in a new role, it made sense for Camile and I to merge our skills to make the maximum amount of money. We were a team because she was at the club making money and I was outside the club fishing to bring the money in. We both brought great attributes to the table. Personally, I felt like I was more approachable than Camile when fishing. She was so stone-faced that men didn't want to talk to her and after being in the business so long and getting some work done to her face, she had a *different* look. She had a recognizable face and some men would back off because they've encountered her previously and remembered getting played. Sometimes guys would stroll in and she would call me to come back to the club if I was striking out in finding any customers to bring back. One thing about us, we didn't need each other. We were capable of making big money on our own. We respected each other for that.

Some girls tried to work with us just to be along for the ride but weren't able to contribute anything of their own. When this happened, those girls became our "workers" or one of our "runners". Camile and I naturally became partners and agreed on a 50/50 split of the funds for every transaction. For example, if the customer was charged $50,000 in total, the club would make an hourly rate from the Champagne Room charge, the host would make an hourly rate, and the club would make money from the bottle service. If the dancers made $40,000, Camile and I would split $30,000 and the other $10,000 was split between the girls that worked for us that night. Camile and I were co-hosts for Lorenzo at this point. I would pick what girls I wanted for my guy. I called the shots and negotiated the price with the customer and Lorenzo.

Camile and I had a love-hate relationship. She and I were definitely "frenemies."We love, we hate, then love each other again. Our innate need to make money and the way we met was what bound us. But both of our desires to control everything was what would separate us. She wanted to control me and I was never going to allow that to happen. She would do some shady shit behind my back like dipping into my cut of the money when I wasn't around. I was good with numbers so I noticed when the money was off. What she failed to understand was I wasn't dumb, young, or green to the life anymore. I was no longer the grasshopper and we weren't dancing in clubs any longer. She carried the same attitude with me in the fishing and credit card escapades as she had in the strip club when I was still dancing. We were past that and she needed to get with the program and respect my newfound role as **her equal.** There was a time when tensions ran high, so Camile and I went our separate ways for a while.

During our break, I ventured out to my old connections and did my own thing. I started doing the same business with another chick I knew named, Erin. Erin and I were able to bring my customers to the clubs. I built my own rapport with the owners of *Scores* and *Penthouse*. I didn't want to bump into Camile at all. I wanted to do my own thing, far away from her. I never made Erin a 50/50 partner because she didn't have as many connections as Camile did. To be honest, Erin was a troublemaker and was fired from every club she worked in. As a matter of fact, I got her fired from *Flashdancers* when she tried to pop shit for no reason. I provoked her in front of the manager and it was over for her from there. She also got fired from *Hustlers* because she was suspected of being a thief. I'd heard she moved on from *Hustlers* and started working at *Penthouse*. Apparently, she was fired from there due to disagreements of some sort. When I ran into her we had a conversation about her working with me. I told her she burned all her bridges, but I'd be willing to work with her. I also told her if I noticed any signs of stealing or any of the bullshit she had going on in the clubs, we were done. She promised to behave and that's how our working relationship was born. I taught her the ropes. I didn't have to train her too much because she was already street smart. The broads Camile hired were airheads and I constantly had to repeat myself. Erin took instruction very well.

One night I went fishing with one of my coworkers, Sonya, instead of taking Erin. Sonya was an older woman, in her 40's if I had to guess. She was also an interesting person. She had plenty of stories about customers but the stories were far-fetched. For example, she said one of her customers bought her a million-dollar apartment on Central Park West. I gave her the benefit of the doubt but put her skills to the test. I wanted her to show me what she was made of. Fishing wasn't easy. We both agreed on going to dinner at Sparks Steakhouse for the night's fishing adventure. We were seated and had normal conversation but kept our eyes open for potential clients with deep pockets. Men would approach us, we'd talk to them briefly, then filter who was worth it. It takes a lot to fish.

Sonya and I finished dinner and walked over to a man that sent me a drink earlier in the evening. I wanted to "thank him" for the drink. His name was Matt, a single, divorced man from Connecticut who was naturally shy. He was about 5'9" with a pudgy, round build. We had a conversation and he told us he was previously a DJ before he got into the insurance business as an adjuster. He did quite well for himself financially. Matt was a nice guy who wasn't a Gentlemen's Club regular. I bet he regrets ever sending me that drink. He didn't have a good poker face and the way he looked at me let me know he was wrapped around my finger. Matt was willing to go wherever I wanted and I wanted to go to the club. I just didn't tell him what *kind* of club. We convinced him to hang out with us and like a puppy, he followed us out to my car. Matt, Sonya, and I jumped in my Escalade and headed to *Hustlers*. When we arrived, I parked my car directly in front of the club, handed my keys to security, and gave the valet $30 to park my truck. As soon as we walked in, Lorenzo was waiting and led us to a private room. I'd texted him back at the restaurant to let him know we were on the way. That ensured there was no waiting period and Matt had no time to think or change his mind. I've had guys hop out my car and leave because they had a bad feeling. Sometimes I'd enable the child locks on my truck to prevent that from happening, then blame the locks on having to keep my daughter safe. I had to stay ahead of the game. However, walking in the club was *their* decision.

I tried to stay out of the private room and let Sonya close the deal, but she said Matt kept asking for me. He was drunk and high off cocaine, sweating and foaming at the corners of his mouth. I wanted Matt to continue coming back so I was polite to him. I didn't want to clean him out completely all in one night. That was Camile's method. She would bleed them dry upfront. I couldn't do that if I wanted him as a client for the long haul so I only charged his card for $8,000 that night. Matt came to me the next day flipping out about the charge. I played dumb and Lorenzo told Matt he'd take care of it. Lorenzo also offered Matt a free bottle of champagne his next visit. That was the perfect way to keep him coming back and it worked! He forgot all about the bill and just like that he became a regular.

Another customer I had was on the verge of purchasing an MLB team. I met him at Le Bernardin. We talked and enjoyed each other's company. I told him I wanted to take him somewhere that he'd never been to. He agreed and I escorted him to *Penthouse*, a strip club that looked like a fancy nightclub. The sign didn't have the club name on it. It had a classy, white swirl design surrounded by big white lights. It had the look of an exclusive member's only lounge. Erin met me outside the club and walked in with us. After looking around, he admitted to never having been there before. *Penthouse* was a ghost town that night. I called the host ahead of time, as I always did, to make sure there was an available room. We walked directly to an empty room and got the party started. We drank, laughed, and sang. It was just another night. We charged his card and without taking a second look, he signed the bill. It was the easiest money I'd ever made and Erin was happy to be making that kind of money again.

I had a growing list of clients and needed to run money through the clubs. While Camile was doing her thing at *Scores* and *Penthouse*, I wanted to stay low key. One day, I got wind of a DJ I knew that worked at *Lace* had passed away. While at the funeral, I ran into Angelo Rossi, the General Manager at *Lace*. He was now running a strip club called, *Roadhouse*. He invited me to come, not knowing I was way past my dancing days. Then, a light went off in my head and Angelo became *my* connect. I explained how my operation worked and he was on board. So I got to work at Angelo's spot with my own girls and my own clients. I used my own merchant transaction process and my consignment business to assist with the money. The operation was running easy and smoothly, which I preferred. The money was clearing and I was still getting paid. I liked small operations and the fewer people, the better.

If Camile thought I needed her, she'd better think again. Apparently, she heard that I was getting money on my own. She's greedy and always wanted a piece of the pie. Everyone has something that makes them tick. A habit, a vice, or a specific taste for something. Hers was money. Having her own wasn't enough, she needed a cut of yours, too. Camile and I split up and got back together a lot. Each time I left her and came back, she'd have a little bit more respect for me. But her old ways would resurface again. I had to talk myself into tolerating her until I was done with this world. I knew I'd hear from her and like clockwork, my phone rang and it was Camile on the other end, wondering if we could get back to making money together. I should have kept it moving but I wasn't one to turn down money so I took her up on her offer and we were back at it.

I had a decent Rolodex of clients that would spend money with us. When a customer would spend a lot of money, I'd move on to the next one. This would allow them enough time to pay their credit card bill. No one likes a pushy salesman, so I wouldn't contact the same client too often. I would rotate the clients which kept us working and in business. I had good "above water" relationships with these men. I would cold call them just to say "hello". Some of them knew about my daughter and would ask about her. Sometimes the client and I exchanged parenting advice. I know it sounds crazy but that was a part of the operation. I didn't treat my customers like "marks". I actually leveled with them personally. It was what I liked to call, the ***Sweet Hustle***. I was approachable, personable, and friendly to get what I wanted. That kept me in the back of their minds when it was time for some unwinding and entertainment. The idea was always to be the sexy laid back chick who's attentive and caring. I had to make these men feel like I was a regular girl with no ulterior motive. I'd ask normal questions like, "What's your favorite color, What's your favorite type of cuisine, etc..." Once a man got comfortable with me, it was easy from there. In a nutshell, that's what the sweet hustle was about; getting what you wanted without them detecting your goal. A lot of these men were in relationships or marriages but lonely, broken and needing companionship. See, I had a more in-depth perspective on what we were doing. This wasn't just about making money by *any* means necessary. It was about relationship building with my clientele; providing a high-quality experience in exchange for the maximum amount of money. We needed to keep a low profile and when you have a team of people who understand that concept, you have a smoother operation.

We recruited women either from the strip club or *Backpage.com* to entertain our customers. *Backpage* was a well-known website for prostitutes which was later seized in April 2018 by the Feds. These women were making less money, getting guerilla pimped, and endangering themselves. They didn't always know what kind of situation they were walking into, literally. They could've been beaten, raped, or even killed. They made more money working with me. Our operation ensured their safety. What more could you ask for in an industry like this? Everything we did was on a sophisticated level; not like your average streetwalker on the corner. I took them under my wing, taught them, and felt like I was saving them. I gave them a better option, whether or not they took advantage of my offer. I guaranteed them $500-$1,000 per night; just about the same rate we got paid when we were just dancing. I picked them up from their homes, made sure they were in safe environments while working, and brought them back when the night was over. Some will say I was their pimp and took their power. However, I didn't see it that way. I was being Captain Save-A-Hoe and they always had a choice. I didn't think I was adding to their pain. We were all there to make money at the end of the day.

One of the girls I recruited from *Backpage* was Tara, who lived in Washington Heights. One night, Camile and I were with a customer at a hotel, drinking and partying with him. The night was ending and we needed a closer. We went to *Backpage* and picked Tara, who we found out was sent by a Russian-owned agency. She came, did what we asked, and we paid her. We also sat and had an honest conversation with her. We asked questions about her experience in the escort world. We were deeply intrigued because we were transitioning from just dancers to madams. We were shocked to hear her stories and the things she went through for such little money. She told us a story about having to climb through a man's bedroom window because he lived at home with his mother. She expressed how afraid she was sometimes of not knowing where she was going for the night and her fear of getting raped or killed. There were times when she wasn't sure she would get paid. I hadn't realized just how crazy being an escort was until she told us about her experience. She was getting paid $100 from the agency and we paid her $300 cash. We told her we'd hire her, ensure her safety by picking her up from home and dropping her back off. In addition to that, we offered her a flat rate of $500 cash at the end of each night. Bottom line, we made her an offer she couldn't refuse.

Working with the girls we recruited, I noticed a pattern. They'd work, make money, then disappear. Later on, I came to understand why. When I asked Tara why she would make money and disappear, she told me it was because she was in the hospital recovering from getting beat up from some guy she was dating. The abuse she endured affected her ability to work. I needed my girls to work; otherwise, I had to find new workers and train them. That was risky because then they knew our operation and word could've gotten out which was bad for business. Not to mention the attempt of copying what we were doing. Tara was a product of her environment. I offered to help her and I gave her an incentive to come to work for us. I offered to cosign for a car and an apartment for her. All she had to do was consistently come to work and I would help her get out of her neighborhood. But she couldn't keep a consistent work schedule. That's when Camile had to hire other workers.

Another one of the girls we hired told me a story about how she met a guy who contacted her because he'd seen her ad on *Backpage*. She met up with the client thinking it was just another night and another guy. After she slept with him she wanted her money. He refused to pay her and the argument escalated. He beat her and broke her jaw, then left her there.

There was another incident when one of the girls met up with a client. They were scheduled to meet at a motel. As they were getting intimate, there was a knock on the door. In walks, another guy and she felt uncomfortable about this. She then gathered her belongings and tried to leave. The two men grabbed her and forced her to the bed. She was raped and left there.

Another time, a girl was sent to a client by her "so-called boyfriend". She was sent there to sleep with him and collect the money. She arrived at the upscale highrise building and was in awe. She said, "Wow, this guy is loaded and I hope he pays me a lot." She sat and drank with the client, as she normally did. Then she began to feel "woozy". She only had one drink and couldn't understand how she was getting drunk so fast. She blacked out and then woke up. The guy convinced her that he didn't owe her anything but she was convinced he violated her. She begged and pleaded for him to pay her. She told him, "I need the money, my boyfriend is going to hurt me." She was scared she was going to get beat up by her boyfriend if she came home empty-handed. She said the last time she didn't pay, he threw her down the stairs and she twisted her ankle. Based on the story she told, her "boyfriend" sounded like a pimp to me.

Some may be wondering what made me take a chance on these girls. It's because I have also been in dire straits and needed someone to have mercy on me; take a chance on me even when all I had to give, was my word. When I was 16 and needed a place to live, I picked up a local newspaper and began my search. I circled some places that were within my budget and went to see them. I was interested in this basement apartment that was owned by a gentleman. I was honest with him about my situation and he gave me a chance by renting it to me. Everyone needs someone to believe in them. Sometimes all you need is an opportunity to prove yourself. These women were in tough situations that required someone reaching out and offering them a solution to their problem. It was my turn to pay it forward. But to be clear, I gave *one* chance to each girl. She had to show me how responsible she was. Some of the girls I offered my help, squandered the opportunity. You can lead 'em to water, but you can't make 'em drink. Everyone isn't worth saving. Some don't even want to be saved.

Working at the pace we were, we definitely had to keep an organized list of old and new clients with notes attached to each name. The notes would hold pertinent information such as, where we met the client, how much they spent on a particular day, where they were employed, and what position they held at that company. The strip club clientele was shrinking, so we had to come up with new creative ways to gain a consistent flow of customers and retain them.

There were four key components of *Operation Sophistication*:

1. Get the customers in the door.
2. Get the customers to spend at least $10,000 per night.
3. Keep the customers entertained.
4. Deal with "chargebacks".

One time, I had a chargeback in the amount of $10,500. We charged the client and the checks were cut. Per usual, everyone got paid. I deposited my check into my bank account but the client disputed the charge and won the dispute. I went to look at my account as I did every day and saw I was missing $10,500. I was in shock and called Camile who informed me that she hadn't cashed her check yet. She never deposited her checks. She always went to a check-cashing spot. She went to a check-cashing spot and got her cut, but she did have to pay it back the same way everyone else did. We took a huge loss. Many times, a customer isn't pissed thinking he was robbed. Usually, the excuse was, *Oh my god, I was drunk!* Classic buyer's remorse. We couldn't get our time back but they damn sure got their money back. There are tons of rewards in this business but the risk was unable to be calculated. It didn't happen often because we stayed on top of everything by always making sure we got a signature and a thumbprint next to the signature; plus the customer was on camera walking in and out of the club willingly. That's difficult to dispute but some of them would definitely try.

Meet Brian, a real estate investor from Nebraska. He was the nicest client I'd ever encountered. Brian always came bearing gifts like luxury handbags, watches, or a shopping spree at Saks. Brian's call meant a guaranteed $5,000 and when he came to town, he'd invite us to his hotel room. He always stayed at the Waldorf Astoria, which wasn't the nicest hotel but it was a classic. Camile and I were always the first ones to go to his room. We never wanted to overwhelm a client when they're sober by bringing too many girls. Once he got a little cocaine in his system, the plan was in motion. We'd call one of the girls to come up, telling the client she was there to bring more cocaine. Typically, when the client saw the girl, he'd want to invite her to stay. By then there's 3-4 of us in the room with the client. When the client was having a good time, either Camile or I would ask for the credit card. Once we had the card, we'd leave and let the girls do the rest. For this particular client, we'd buy condoms, KY Jelly, and a dildo. This one liked to have champagne bottles shoved up his ass. I've seen and heard a lot so I try not to judge. We're there to provide an experience for him.

Once we worked out the minor details, Camile and I became the dream team, like Kobe and Shaq. We won championships together but had some personal differences on the court. Camile amazed me sometimes, she just knew what to do. Where she lacked in one area, I picked up and vice versa. Camile and I bounced off of each other quite a bit. We would unknowingly play, Good Cop/Bad Cop with the girls we employed. Sometimes these broads could piss me off something serious. Camile would have to calm me down and pull the girl to the side, straighten her out and vice versa.

Camile and I were getting along pretty well at this point. Even in our disagreements, one thing we always agreed on was money is green; it didn't matter who had it, we took it. But we were both alpha females with strong personalities. However, I knew I was better than the others; I just couldn't act like a snob. If I had, that would've compromised the work we were doing and everyone played a vital role. We didn't have time for anyone to be flexin'. I looked at her as an equal and I thought she did the same. That was the difference between Camile and I. There were moments when I noticed she didn't respect my opinion. It seemed as though she assumed she was above me and I wasn't going for that. Did she put me on? Yes. Did she have more years under her belt in the game than me? Yes and I respected her, but this wasn't about seniority. I put in the same amount of work as she did. She had connections that came in handy and she definitely knew how to work her resources but so did I. We were equally taking the same risk.

The girls were recruited to entertain the men while Camile and I did the behind-the-scenes work. We were even fair to the "dirty girls." Once we squeezed the customer for everything we possibly could, we would send in the "dirty girls" at the end to give the customer whatever sexual favor they were hoping for. They would get something like $500 out of the deal. This way everybody made money. We never stole anything. We paid the girls a decent amount of money per night and they were satisfied with that. This was all business for us and if it was a legit business, Camile, would've been the CEO and I would've been the CFO. That's how it worked. We didn't play games when it came to the cash flow. Word in the strip club world was Camile and I were killing it. We were bringing in big numbers every night. It became increasingly difficult to work with the host at *Hustlers*. We seemed to have disagreements about payout amounts. He wasn't giving us the amounts we felt we deserved. We had our clients, we knew how much we could get them to spend, and we even had our own drugs and workers. We decided to seek other places to work. Working as an independent contractor meant we were able to work at other clubs and take our clients to any club. Now that we were running our own operation, we called the shots...ALL of them. We had an extraordinary operation and we wanted to switch to a club that would do right by us.

If we had big numbers and low chargeback ratings, why wouldn't you want to partner with us? When you're in one place for too long, people don't appreciate you like they used to. It felt like *Hustlers* was no longer appreciative of the business we were bringing in. It was time to rise above the bullshit and take our business elsewhere. Camile got *Scores* to accept us as independent contractors and I was able to get *Roadhouse* to cut us checks as well. That's what it's about; **bringing the clients, running the cards, and cutting the check.**

I called the credit card company, the custy verified his information, then he allowed me to get on the phone and take over from there.

CHAPTER 10

The Hustlers At Scores

Scores was our new spot. We walked in the club through the back door with our clients and straight to the Champagne Room. This made the client feel exclusive. *Scores* allowed us to run big money as long as we didn't have any chargebacks. A chargeback was equal to having a mark on your report card; it caused a lot of problems including losing trust in the eyes of the owner and the money having to be paid back. We didn't need that kind of negative reputation. We were putting our asses on the line to make the money.

Working at *Scores* was a breath of fresh air from *Hustlers*. Much like, when I left *Flashdancers* and went to *Hustlers*. Every new spot was always a step up or so I thought. In the dancing world, not everyone respected dancers. We, as dancers, had to demand our pay and what was fair to us. We did all the work and if we weren't respected, we simply took our business elsewhere. Wherever we went, our clients followed. We were Free Agents and at the end of the day, we knew what we brought to the table and we knew our worth. We grew more powerful and had more leverage; that, combined with talent, there was nowhere to go from here but up.

As CFO, I was in charge of the financial dealings, such as finding out the available daily amount that could be charged so we didn't raise any fraud alerts or block the credit card. It was also my job to find out if there was a block on the card, such as, from a high balance that needed to be paid before the next charge would go through. I would call the credit card company, the custy would verify his information, then he would allow me to get on the phone and take over from there. We would do this after drinks, drugs, and hot girls were in his presence and he was feeling nice. When I was on the phone with the credit card company, I would ask them to do a test run since many of the cards like Amex didn't have a set limit. The limits were personalized based on an average of spending; this determined whether or not the charge would go through. This was my way of making sure the card didn't get declined because when it did, the customer had to get on the phone and verify the $10,000 charge that was just declined. This was how we avoided blowing our cover.

As the CEO, Camile was in charge of the girls and which girl to pair with each customer. The girls were given specific details on how to deal with the customer and what to do once they were in the Champagne Room. She seemed to know almost everyone in this industry since she began dancing around 18 and was now in her 40's. She was well-known in the NYC nightlife as a dancer and socialite. We worked well together and we each played our roles well. We were a one-stop-shop when it came to entertaining the high rollers.

In order to continue bringing business to the club, we had a deal with the owner and allowed some of his dancers to make money along with us. We walked in as an entourage. It was Camile, myself, a trusted top worker, and an additional girl. There were levels to our operation. We only kept four girls working for us at a time. It was easier to manage a minimal amount of people. Not only that, we didn't have to split money too many different ways. Each person was being watched so they wouldn't take the guy's phone number and call him directly to make some side money. Even if this did happen, the girls could never get the kind of money we got. They didn't have the credit card processing capabilities. Ninety-five percent of the clients didn't carry a lot of cash on them, they were all credit card guys. So, our girls weren't able to circumvent our system and had to stick to our rules.

Sometimes, the girls would come to me for guidance or advice and while the thought is endearing now, I was harsh with them at the time. Maybe even downright mean. What we were doing was serious and there was no room for silly hiccups. Some of the things they stumbled over were minor issues. These were adult women who should have been able to use their own minds and better judgment. I didn't have patience for the bullshit. I laid out the game for them in detail and simplicity. They had fuzzy logic and that annoyed me. We had a strong operation going and some of the girls would get caught up in the hype, drinking and partying, and forget that we had an ultimate mission. My thoughts were, *keep your shit together, get the money, and go home*.

Once, we hired a transgender who sent me pictures of the client with a dildo in his ass. See, that's the kind of bullshit I didn't need to know about or see. Just do the job and get out. The way you chose to get down was solely your business. But the pictures did come in handy. If the customer threatened us with a chargeback on their credit card, Camile would threaten them with the pictures. It's a dirty game, but we had to protect ourselves. We were already taking a penitentiary chance with the credit cards. The last thing we needed was blowback with the cards and not making the money. That wasn't an option. We had to come out on top; no exceptions. Camile had no soul and was ruthless. She had a fucked up way of doing things and I wasn't always in cahoots with her methods but what choice did I have when her ways worked? She was in the game longer than me. By now, she had something like 20 years in the business. Of course, she didn't have a heart for these men.

I remember watching the movie, *American Gangster.* I noticed how Frank Lucas moved within his organization. Quiet and not at all flashy. He always noticed the clown in the room with unbearable amounts of arrogance, boasting, and bringing a lot of unnecessary attention to themselves knowing they were heavily involved in illegal activity. You can't be wildin', buying unnecessary expensive pieces; especially if they scream EXPENSIVE and bring too much attention to yourself. That makes you a target. No, you don't have to be a bum, but you can carry a Gucci without anyone knowing its a Gucci. **Discretion.** That was the name of the game. At the fastest rate, Camile was getting beside herself acting as though she was invincible. I tried to reel her in but I was losing my grip on her mind. She was getting sloppy and greedy. She brought me into this method of getting money. I was confused and pissed at the 180° turn she'd taken. We swapped roles and the student was now becoming the teacher. This game is snake-like. Cut off the head of the snake and another will grow in its place. I couldn't risk everything we built because of her lack of caution. All of this was not for nothing. So I stood up and took my rightful place in the operation as *the Madam.*

Keeping a tight-knit operation is key to any organization. We had a lot of issues to deal with. For example, we had to deal with the owners when there was a dispute about a charge. We had to deal with the clients before and after the transaction. We dealt with the host about how much to run the card for after checking the available credit line. We had to deal with the payroll of each dancer and worker. Sometimes we had to increase their pay because they heard about the kind of money we took home after charging the customer. Naturally, they wanted more money. We had to deal with buying and mixing the drugs. It was a lot and the more people involved, the more things got out of control.

Working in this industry was a vicious cycle but I really ran this ring like a business. I had a child to support and financial goals to achieve. I wanted to make as much money as possible and get out. However, not everything in life works out the way you've planned. We had a good thing going until things got out of hand. I'm big on trust and loyalty so we had to have a ring of the same workers and not allow newcomers into our circle. Not only were we concerned about law enforcement but also about our operation being duplicated by someone else. Camile trusted too many girls and allowed stragglers into the fold. Stragglers were the ones that were drug addicts, and the liabilities we didn't need. We clashed about that often. She was always convinced that they would be fine and they'd listen to her. In my opinion, the strays had no one because they'd already burned their bridges. Camile only wanted them around to have control over them. My thought process was, *what do we want with them?* I warned Camile that people like them bring trouble and will get us caught…and that's what happened.

Lo and behold, one of Camile's stragglers caught a drug charge separately from us. She was a junkie and later I found out she became an informant. This led to an investigation of my associates and I. Due to the deal I took with the DEA, I can't go into detail about this, but my decision to be a hustler wasn't easy. I **always** followed my gut. My relationship with Camile drastically changed towards the end of our reign. Something told me this entire business operation between us was going to go left. This was the *one time*, I didn't follow my gut. **I allowed greed to control me.**

All it takes is one person in the organization to slip up, make the loud, obvious mistake, and cause everything to come crashing down. That was

Camile and her love for strays. One night, we are at the scene of a financial transaction sitting in my white Escalade trying to make sure everything ran smoothly and there she sat, oblivious, on her iPad scrolling through the Gucci website. I was completely and utterly annoyed with her. She wasn't focused. She seemed to have her head in the clouds and I needed to snatch it back, fast! Don't get me wrong, we had plenty of designer clothes, jewelry, and nice cars from our dancing days. But that was at a time when we were legit.

Since the business changed, naturally, the rules changed, too. I don't know what she didn't understand about that because it was common sense to me. I no longer trusted her and I began to resent her for the decisions she was making. We were having issues and I noticed she no longer valued my opinion and started trying to run the operation on her own. There were times when the money would fall through; maybe a customer wouldn't verify the charge and we'd have to take the loss. Her spending habits, mixed with her greed, and complete negligence of what was at stake, was convincing me that **this was no longer a sophisticated hustle.** Getting caught is not what I signed up for. Honestly, I wanted out long before the investigation started. I'd watched enough episodes of *The Sopranos* to foresee the destruction coming.

Meet Nikki, a dancer from *Scores*, who was considered a "dirty girl" and a certified junkie. I never liked this girl from the moment I met her. I'm all about energy because it doesn't lie. She gave me bad vibes but for some reason, Camile always vouched for her, always felt bad for her, and allowed her to work with us. Here we go again with her love for strays. On top of being a prime drug user, she was a poor parent and as a result, her son was taken away from her. As a mother, that rubbed me the wrong way. I always liked to see how people treated their kids, friends, and family. In my opinion, that spoke about your character. In the beginning, I mentioned wanting to associate myself with people who had morals and principles. This is what I was talking about. I wanted good people on my team; people who understood loyalty and respect for their coworkers, family, and friends. Looking back at it all, I wanted too much from the wrong people and tried to get that in the wrong line of work. I'll never forget, my lawyer once told me, "Rosie, there is no honor among thieves." I learned this the hard way.

I knew some shit was about to go down and I wanted out! This whole thing was getting out of hand. Word got out that I was quitting and moving to Miami. That's when I got picked up by the authorities. Thanks to my associate, Camile, who brought Natalie into the fold, she set me up during a sting operation. I hired a lawyer before I was even indicted. I wanted to see how much dirt they had on me and what my options were. I knew I couldn't trust anyone in the ring. When you're talking about compromising your freedom, it was every man for themselves. Besides, I was the only one with a toddler to think about. Camile had a son who was 18 at the time. I felt I had more to lose than her. At this point, I was at my wit's end with the way things were going. My resentment for everyone had grown extensively over the years due to the lies, deceit, and drama. One major question I asked myself throughout the decision of whether or not to cooperate with the authorities was, "Would these girls go to bat for you?" No, I didn't think they would. My lawyer's words replayed in my mind over and over again, "Rosie, there is no honor among thieves." I decided to cooperate, signed an agreement, and can't say too much else because of it.

There is a lot of biased information out there about my associates and I. We were portrayed as the "bad guys" when the story broke publicly. Many of our clients were already drug users and repeat customers prepared to splurge on entertainment. They sniffed cocaine and drank alcohol just like everyone else. All we did was slip them a little extra by mixing in Molly with the cocaine they were already using. We didn't twist any arms or place guns to anyone's head. In my mind, it was all consensual. This was what came with the territory, right? To say that we "drugged" these men, as if they were innocent, is laughable. The men willingly engaged in having a good time with the girls and we got paid as a result. We were an escape for them from their highly stressful jobs, nagging wives, families, and daily responsibilities. On both sides, no one was innocent.

I played soccer growing up which kept me in shape and built my level of endurance as an athlete. It also made me the jogger I am today. Being an athlete has taught me to never give up and always work hard to get what I want. I was competitive and I looked at every night of work as a competition. It was like a game of "who can make the most money?" It felt good to be on top and always be able to say, R.I.P. to the competition. I was definitely an alpha female. This is probably the reason I would clash with other alpha females like Camile. We'd work well together in the beginning, then she tried to take too much control or give me orders. I wasn't taking any shit. I'm tough and a fighter. Back then, I didn't mind if we had to throw down.

I had a tough upbringing that shaped who I was for a long time. I was trapped inside the mind of a hurting little girl and I couldn't get out. Consequently, all the years of disrespect and pain I went through, triggered anger, my revenge on men, and whoever sought to bring me trouble. I was a spiteful, vengeful person and I set out to one day get retribution for the hurt others caused me. The interesting thing about pain is everyone experiences it but handles it differently. Oprah once said, "Hurt people, hurt people..." I was hurt and it made me feel good to hurt others. **I can't believe what a hot head I was.** I'm no longer that hurt girl and I forgive everyone that has hurt me in the past. I learned that when I harbored my anger and pain, it did me more harm than my enemy. These days, I believe it's better to take the high road and turn the other cheek when it comes to the bullshit. I found that the best revenge is to move on, do well for myself, and be successful. Knowing that people who don't care for you see it or hear about it from afar is a bonus!

It's unfortunate that it took an incident so drastic to happen in order for me to make a change in my life. Getting arrested was a dark moment in my life but it was also a pivotal moment in my **DESTINY**. It brought me back to reality and made me change my life completely. I have to look at my arrest as a blessing in disguise and a lesson learned. I had a choice to make. I could've let it get the best of me, making me bitter. But I decided to learn and grow from it and allow it to make me a better woman. In life, you can't let your situation define who you are. Improvement and redemption are possible. You just have to believe in your own ability, want change, and work toward becoming a better you. Contrary to popular belief, every situation I was caught in was just me trying to better myself in some capacity. Even with all the mental abuse I endured as a child and the dysfunctional relationships I engaged in, I knew I was better than that. I wanted more out of my life. I had to believe that I wasn't what they said I was. I was also determined to show and prove. With a little self-love and avoiding negative people and unhealthy environments, everything started falling into place.

If you know me, you know I have an extreme personality; the crazy, sexy, and cool type. It's all or nothing with me and that caused me to learn everything the hard way. The money I made back then was addictive but it wasn't reality. I couldn't do it forever. I walked into an uneasy environment blindly, thinking I was strong enough mentally to not allow it to swallow me up. I didn't think my previous lifestyle would get the best of me but little by little, it did. I looked at the other dancers and always thought to myself, *Don't let that be you.* What I've learned in the midst of all this chaos is that there's is a fine line between ambition and greed. Money comes and goes; to chase it, is nothing more than foolish. The indictment brought my lifestyle to a screeching halt. It was a rude awakening from God telling me that I needed to stop and refocus my energy and efforts on my daughter and live my life the way I should've been all along. The universe will send out signs and signals when necessary to grab your attention. I *knew* better but I got greedy in my efforts to establish myself financially so that my daughter would have a better life than I had.

I was so adamant about making money to sustain myself that I forgot to love myself along the way. Everything was about the hustle and if it wasn't, then I was less than interested. Healthy self-love definitely wasn't high on my list of priorities. I found that real love in any form comes from within; who cares what people think? I always felt that I had people to prove wrong. But their thoughts of me didn't pay my bills. Yet, I had to tell my truth. It was difficult to be this transparent and open, uncovering memories that I buried long ago, and digging up things I didn't want to face or confront again. I was afraid that my truth would drag me back into a deep depression. I was previously diagnosed with bipolar disorder and manic depression. I couldn't bear the thought of carrying on sometimes which fostered frequent thoughts of suicide. In those moments, I thought it would be easier to die rather than live a life of constant pain. I found out that depression is a hereditary illness. According to The National Alliance on Mental Health, Approximately 1 in 5 adults in the U.S. (46.6 million) experiences mental illness in a given year. My father's side of the family had a history of depression and I had family members who committed suicide. When I was young, I'd often tell my mom I had these thoughts and she'd always downplay me saying, "Ugh, you get that from your daddy's side." In a sense she was right. But not only did my dad's side have a history of mental illness, so did my mom's side. A family member on my mom's side was diagnosed with Schizophrenia. Nevertheless, I'm not here to play the victim and blame the results of my decisions solely on depression or my childhood pain. I'm here to say what doesn't kill you will make you smarter and stronger. Everything in life is a learning lesson. Everyone makes poor choices. It's through those lessons learned from those choices that mold you into a better human being.

It's never too late to change. In my case, getting arrested and finally coming out of the strip club world gave me clarity. I realized that money wasn't everything. The decision I made to change my life and focus on my daughter made me a better person. My main job is raising her the way I *wanted* to be raised. Now, I hustle hard for the PTA. Without exception, I volunteer my time and stay involved with her school activities. It makes her happy to see me engaged in her school. After I was diagnosed with a mental illness, I began taking medication to control the disease which made me feel crazier than the actual diagnosis. I didn't want to be dependent on the medication so I stopped taking it. I needed to find other ways to create and nurture happiness for myself. I fell in love with fitness. Working out at the gym after I see my daughter off to school has created happiness for me; mind, body, and soul. It's been scientifically proven that fitness creates happy endorphins in the brain. I'm living proof of this. I've come a long way mentally and I wish I knew then what I know now. As a result of my personal happiness, I'm equipped to guide my daughter down the right path. I always said I could have been something really great if my parents took care of me properly and I didn't have to worry about money or raising myself. But such is life. It could've been worse. You just have to condition your mind to count your blessings, not your problems.

About The Sophisticated Hustler

Roselyn Keo, a New York native, was born and raised in a small county 20 minutes from Manhattan. Not coming from much she worked hard to support herself. She attended college at Berkeley in New York City. From slinging plates at a local diner to swinging on the poles in the Big Apple, she got into dancing at 17-years-old. She eventually learned the art of hustling from a young age and through all her life experiences. Rosie always dreamed big, constantly wanting better.

At the age of 27, when the game had changed, she changed the game; which landed her behind bars. This was a blessing in disguise, which she did not realize until later. She has learned many life lessons the hard way. With every curve ball thrown at her, she always remained true to herself, remaining undefeated. She learned the power of resilience, leadership and the importance of family. Being an amazing mother to her daughter has been the most important job she has ever taken on. Maintaining a happy and healthy lifestyle while being a stay at home mom has been quite rewarding for Roselyn and her family. After years of hiding from her past, she discovered that a movie inspired by her life story was in the making. Instead of allowing Hollywood to narrate a version of who she truly is, she decided to take charge and tell her version of what truly happened. **Meet The Sophisticated Hustler—Roselyn Keo.**

Printed in Poland
by Amazon Fulfillment
Poland Sp. z o.o., Wrocław

53125859R00065